AWKWARD
CORNERS

AWKWARD CORNERS

TURNING EYESORES INTO BEAUTY SPOTS

ALAN TOOGOOD

WARD LOCK LIMITED · LONDON

© Ward Lock Ltd., 1988.

First published in Great Britain in 1988
by Ward Lock Limited, 8 Clifford Street,
London W1X 1RB, an Egmont Company.

House editor Denis Ingram.
Designed by Anne Sharples.
Text filmset in Optima Series by Facet Film Composing Ltd., Leigh-on-Sea, Essex.
Printed and bound in Italy by Canale

British Library Cataloguing in Publication Data.
Toogood, Alan R., *1941*
    Awkward corners: turning eyesores into
beauty.
    1. Gardening
    I. Title
    635

ISBN 0-7063-6705-7

CONTENTS

INTRODUCTION

Boring, lifeless corners, where nothing seems to grow, are often found in small town gardens. Perhaps it is the design of the major garden features like the lawn, patio, beds and borders which inadvertently results in these little problem areas.

Large-garden owners rarely seem to have awkward corners – or perhaps because of the size of the garden they do not detract from the overall effect and can therefore be ignored. However, in the small town garden even a square foot of ground can be unsightly unless it is well planted or improved in some other way. In any case, the small-garden owner simply cannot afford to waste space – every odd corner is valuable.

Corners are created by such things as boundary walls and fences, the house walls and perhaps the walls of outbuildings like the garage, shed and so on. Often, surprisingly perhaps, they are considered awkward or difficult places to cope with and indeed they can present garden owners with a diverse range of conditions. Some corners are gloomy or shady. Others have soil which is either like a bog or a desert: very wet or extremely dry. Then there are corners which suffer a lot of wear, so much so that it is difficult or impossible to grow plants. In some corners there may be difficult shapes, such as extremely narrow borders or even part of a steep bank. You may have planted some corners yet do not manage to achieve colour for more than a few weeks each year so they appear dull for much of the time.

None of these problems is insurmountable, and indeed there are dozens of ideas in my book for making such corners attractive features in their own right. One need not use only plants: there are garden ornaments and statuary, mirrors, lighting, murals, garden-construction materials – and even artificial plants and 'grass' if conditions are so extreme that nothing will grow. I will help you improve the most unlikely corners, so I make no apologies for occasionally dismissing conventional gardening practices and going for quirky effects.

Of course, lots of plants which are suitable for different situations have been listed and described. However, I have steered clear of dull or boring kinds (there are far too many of these in gardens already) as I feel that plants should excite the senses. Therefore, many of the plants that I have chosen for corners are unusual or dramatic – even amusing and bizarre!

There are ideas for complete mini features which fit into odd corners of the garden, including little raised beds, a plant wheel for dwarf or low-growing subjects or herbs, and even mini pools and fountains.

People who like to collect particular types of plants, like alpines, will find ideas for displaying their treasures in corners of the garden.

You will find most of the ideas for brightening up corners quick, easy and economical – there is certainly no need to spend large sums of money (save that for the major garden features).

In addition, as you turn the pages of this book the specially commissioned drawings open out to form actual corners. This, hopefully, will give you a very good idea of what the particular feature will look like when incorporated into your own garden.

A.T.

CHAPTER ONE

BANISHING GLOOM

Shady corners can be rather depressing unless steps are taken to brighten them up. There are plenty of plants that can be used, as well as exciting and unusual man-made objects and materials.

CLIMBERS AND OTHER PLANTS

Here is considered a wide range of shade-loving plants for colour and interest all year round.

———

PLANTS IN CONTAINERS

A collection of ornamental containers in a corner could be planted with colourful shade-loving plants.

———

MIRRORS AND STATUES

A large mirror mounted on a wall will reflect light and create the illusion of depth. And light-coloured statuary also helps to brighten up a dark dingy corner.

There is a surprisingly wide range of plants suitable for shady corners, including climbers for walls and fences, shrubs and perennials.

Although despised by many gardeners, one should not dismiss the use of artificial or plastic plants, particularly if you want to achieve colour in a very difficult situation. Many are very realistic, especially when combined with real plants. Their value lies in providing colour – and all the year round. I have come across various types of climbers, like ivies, which could be used on walls and fences, and other flowering plants such as hydrangeas.

Some artificial plants are 'exotic', so you could even create a tropical effect in your corner!

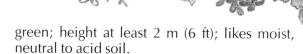

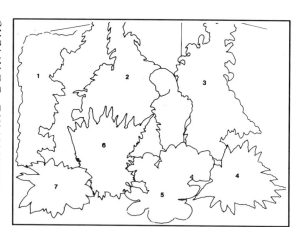

1. *Hedera colchica* Dentata Variegata' (variegated Persian ivy)
2. *Hydrangea petiolaris* (climbing hydrangea)
3. *Actinidia kolomikta* (Kolomikta vine)
4. Ferns
5. Bergenias
6. Astilbes
7. Hostas (plantain lilies)

PLANTS FOR SHADY WALLS

There are lots of climbers and wall shrubs which will provide colour and interest on walls and fences which receive no sun. They could be trained to trellis panels secured to the wall or fence, or to horizontal galvanized wires, spaced about 30 cm (12 in) apart, supported with metal vine eyes. Remember that trellis panels and wires should be held at least 2.5 cm (1 in) away from a wall or fence to allow good air circulation behind the plants.

Actinidia kolomikta (Kolomikta vine) Large deep green foliage liberally 'painted' with pink and white; deciduous, height up to 3.6 m (12 ft); best in partial shade.

Berberidopsis corallina (coral plant) Pendulous crimson flowers in late summer; ever-green; height at least 2 m (6 ft); likes moist, neutral to acid soil.

Celastrus orbiculatus (staff vine) Bright orange and scarlet fruits and yellow foliage in autumn; deciduous; height up to 9 m (30 ft); partial shade.

Chaenomeles speciosa (ornamental quince) Pink, red or white blooms in spring; deciduous; height about 2 m (6 ft).

Clematis The clematis prefer a position where their 'heads' are in the sun and their roots are shaded. There are many large-flowered hybrids for summer flowering, and species like the popular *C. montana* and its varieties, with white or pink flowers in spring. This one will take more shade. Most are deciduous and heights are variable.

Cotoneaster horizontalis (fishbone cotoneaster) Has a flat, fishbone-system of branches which in autumn are laden with red berries; deciduous; height up to 2.4 m (8 ft).

Garrya elliptica This produces long grey-green catkins in winter and looks lovely with winter jasmine (see below); a good variety is 'James Roof'; evergreen; height at least 2.4 m (8 ft).

Hedera (ivy) There are various kinds of ivy to choose from, ideally those with light variegated foliage like many of the *H. helix* forms, or the large-leaved *H. canariensis* 'Gloire de Marengo' and *H. colchica* 'Dentata Variegata'; all are evergreen; heights are variable; they cling to walls and fences without additional support.

Hydrangea petiolaris (climbing hydrangea) Flat heads of white flowers produced in summer; deciduous; height at least 7.5 m (25 ft); clings to walls and fences without additional support.

Jasminum nudiflorum (winter jasmine) Masses

of bright yellow flowers in winter; deciduous; height about 3 m (10 ft).

Parthenocissus quinquefolia (Virginia creeper) The leaves take on bright scarlet and orange tints in autumn; deciduous; tall, but can be winter-pruned; clings to walls and fences without additional support.

Polygonum baldschuanicum (Russian vine) Masses of foamy white flowers in summer/early autumn; deciduous; height up to 12 m (40 ft) but can be cut back in late winter.

Pyracantha (firethorn) There are many species and varieties, with orange, red or yellow berries in autumn, all suitable for shade; evergreen; height up to 3.6 m (12 ft).

Rosa (climbing roses) Several varieties are suitable for shady walls, including 'Aloha', coral pink, 2.4 m (8 ft); 'Danse du Feu', brilliant orange-red, 3 m (10 ft); 'Golden Showers', bright yellow, 2.4 m (8 ft); 'Maigold', golden yellow, 3 m (10 ft); 'New Dawn', palest pink, 1.8 m (6 ft); and 'Sympathie', bright scarlet, 3 m (10 ft). All are deciduous.

DWARF PERENNIALS

Low-growing perennials could be grouped around the base of the climbers to provide colour and foliage interest on a lower level. For instance, a combination of astilbes and hostas (plantain lilies) would look lovely. Astilbes have feathery plumes of flowers in summer, in shades of red, pink or white, and the large bold leaves of hostas come in all shades of green, blue-grey and variegated. Both like reasonably moist soil.

Bergenias have large, bold, evergreen leaves and in the spring produce flower-heads in various shades of pink and also white. Our shady corner is also the ideal place to grow the ever-popular lily-of-the-valley, *Convallaria majalis,* with highly fragrant, white, bell-like flowers in spring.

Hardy ferns of all kinds combine beautifully with any of these perennials. Just take your pick from any of those stocked by garden centres.

HELPFUL HINTS

When planting climbers against a wall or fence bear in mind that they should not be set hard up against the structure. Rather, position each plant about 30 cm (12 in) away from the wall or fence and then guide the stems to the support with bamboo canes angled inwards. This is because immediately in front of a wall or fence the soil generally remains quite dry as rain is deflected by the structure. In these conditions the plants would not establish.

Young climbers should be kept well watered if the soil is dry, until they are well established and growing strongly. In order to conserve moisture around their roots it pays to mulch the plants with organic matter immediately after planting. A 5 cm (2 in) deep layer of peat, pulverized bark or leafmould over the root area will keep the plants happy.

Many people wrongly think that climbing plants, especially ivy, will damage brickwork, but this is not the case provided the brickwork is perfectly sound – as it should be!

I have included ivies (or hederas) in several of my corners and it is worth remembering that they need an annual 'haircut' as they can become very dense and heavy, when they may fall away from their supports. So in mid-spring trim them back hard with garden shears. Afterwards they will look rather bare but will soon re-clothe themselves with foliage.

Plants In Containers

Ornamental containers such as tubs, pots and urns could be clustered in a shady corner and planted with colourful plants.

The advantage of containers is that they can be moved into the corner when the plants are in flower and then transferred to an out-of-the-way part of the garden when they lack colour and interest.

SUMMER COLOUR

To provide colour in the summer there are several bedding plants that perform well in shade. These should be planted when all danger of frost is over, in late spring or early summer. Take your pick from the fibrous-rooted begonias, *Begonia semperflorens,* with masses of small flowers in shades of red, pink and also white, and with green or bronze foliage; bush fuchsias, and trailing kinds for the edges of containers (greenhouse varieties); the bedding impatiens or busy lizzies, which flower profusely throughout summer, in shades of red, pink, orange and white; and bedding mimulus or monkey flower with brilliant blooms in shades of yellow, orange and red.

13

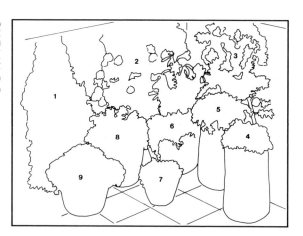

1. *Parthenocissus quinquefolia* (Virginia creeper)
2. Climbing rose 'New Dawn'
3. Pyracantha (firethorn)
4. Mimulus
5. *Euonymus fortunei* variety
6. Variegated ivy with *Lilium regale* (regal lily)
7. *Begonia semperflorens* (wax begonia)
8. Fuchsia
9. Impatiens

Spring colour for containers. From left to right: *Primula denticulata* (drumstick primrose), polyanthus and myosotis (forget-me-nots). The background climbers are parthenocissus and roses.

SPRING COLOUR

There are several spring-flowering bedding plants suitable for shade, which can be planted in the autumn when the summer bedding has been cleared. These include myosotis or forget-me-nots, with clouds of blue flowers; and the polyanthus and coloured primroses, which come in many different colours.

Something more unusual for spring colour is the drumstick primrose, *Primula denticulata*, which has large globular heads of flowers in mauve, shades of pink, purple or white. It is a perennial, so can be left in the containers for several years if desired.

It is worth noting that this primula is easily raised from seeds sown under glass during spring, in moderate heat.

BULBS

Bulbs to provide colour in spring or summer include the snowdrop, *Galanthus nivalis,* with white flowers in winter/early spring; the snake's head fritillary, *Fritillaria meleagris,* with pendulous, bell-shaped, chequered-purple flowers in spring; the miniature cyclamen, *C. hederifolium (C. neapolitanum),* with pink or white flowers in late summer/autumn; and miniature daffodils such as *Narcissus cyclamineus* and its hybrids, and *N. bulbocodium,* all spring flowering.

Some lilies, for summer flowering, do well in containers, particularly *Lilium speciosum, L. auratum* and *L. regale.* Lilies are best in partial shade, rather than a completely sunless position.

All bulbs can be left in their containers as they are permanent subjects, and indeed could be combined with any of the permanent trailing plants described below.

TRAILING PLANTS

Permanent trailing plants, for the edges of containers, reduce the need for a lot of regular replanting and can be combined with temporary bedding plants as well as bulbs.

Varieties of *Ajuga reptans* or bugle often have coloured foliage, particularly 'Variegata' (green and cream) and 'Multicolor' (pink, yellow and bronze). *Euonymus fortunei*

'Variegatus' is a trailing evergreen shrub with greyish-green foliage edged with white. Small-leaved ivies, varieties of *Hedera helix,* especially the light-coloured variegated kinds, would be ideal, too, for the edges of containers. The creeping, mat-forming *Helxine soleirolii* will 'soften' the edges of containers with its minute pale green leaves, or yellow-green in variety 'Aurea'.

Lamium maculatum varieties, or dead nettle, are low spreading perennials. Flowers are pink or white and the variety 'Aureum' has yellow foliage. The lesser periwinkle, *Vinca minor,* is a trailing evergreen with blue, purple or white flowers in spring.

PLANTS FOR VERY DEEP SHADE

Very deep shade, for example often found in the narrow passageways between houses, calls for some very tolerant, tough shrubs. They should also be tolerant of windy conditions, for such passageways are often prone to wind funnelling. Corners of basement gardens can also be cast in deep shade. Try the following shrubs in these situations.

Aucuba japonica (spotted laurel) Large-leaved evergreen shrub, heavily spotted with yellow in the varieties 'Crotonifolia', 'Gold Dust', 'Picturata' and 'Variegata'. Height over 2 m (6 ft).

Buxus sempervirens 'Elegantissima' (box) Small-leaved evergreen shrub with white-edged leaves; slow growing; height 1–1.5m (3–5 ft).

Euonymus fortunei Evergreen shrub. Choose bushy varieties with variegated foliage, such as 'Emerald and Gold', 1 m (3 ft) high; 'Silver Pillar', 1.8–2.4 m (6–8ft); and 'Silver Queen', similar height.

Mahonia aquifolium (Oregon grape) Although this evergreen shrub has rather sombre, deep green foliage, it produces, in spring, long-lasting clusters of scented yellow flowers. Height up to 1.5 m (5 ft).

Prunus laurocerasus 'Marbled White' ('Variegata') (cherry laurel) A variety heavily variegated with white and grey-green. Large evergreen foliage; slow-growing to over 3 m (10 ft) in height.

Symphoricarpos (snowberry) Tough adaptable shrubs, most attractive in the autumn and winter when covered with white berries. The best one for berries is *S. rivularis. S. × doorenbosii* 'Mother of Pearl' has large white berries flushed with pink.

These shrubs can be grown in ornamental containers if desired, which means that they can be moved around and displays changed as required. For instance, flowering plants could be brought into the area while at their best, and later moved to an out-of-the-way part of the garden.

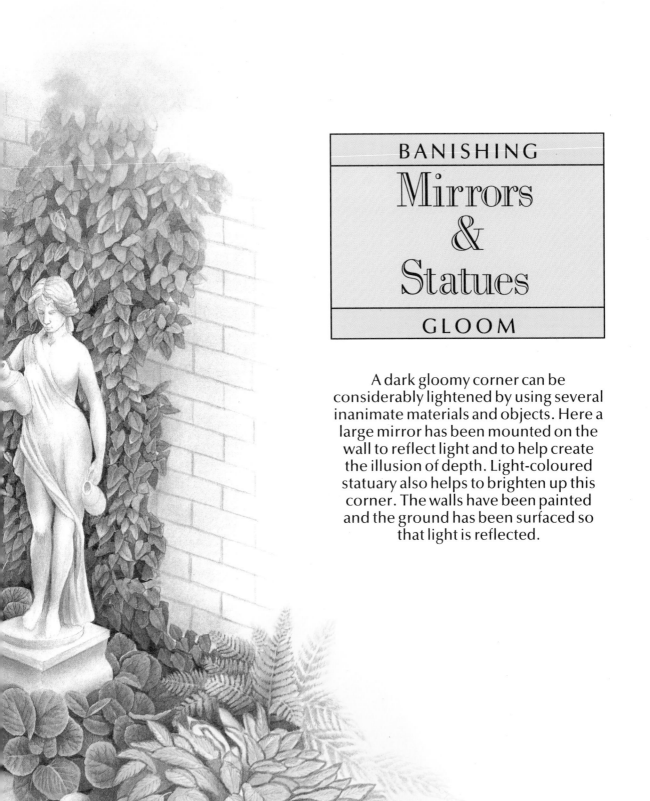

BANISHING
Mirrors
&
Statues
GLOOM

A dark gloomy corner can be considerably lightened by using several inanimate materials and objects. Here a large mirror has been mounted on the wall to reflect light and to help create the illusion of depth. Light-coloured statuary also helps to brighten up this corner. The walls have been painted and the ground has been surfaced so that light is reflected.

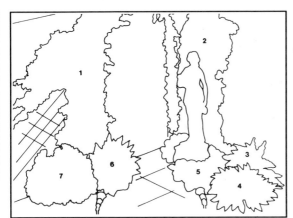

1. *Clematis montana*
2. *Hedera colchica* (Persian ivy)
3. Ferns
4. Hostas (plantain lilies)
5. Bergenias
6. Ferns
7. *Euonymus fortunei* variety

PAINTING

Walls and fences can be painted to help brighten up a corner. Light-coloured paint such as white, cream or pastel green will help to reflect light and so make a dark corner more inviting.

Brick or concrete walls should be painted with a good quality masonry paint, ideally one which contains a quantity of very fine sand as this lasts for many years before it needs renewing. It pays to prepare the wall well before painting it by making good any crumbling mortar and filling in any holes with mortar. Then apply stabilizing solution (masonry type) according to the maker's instructions: when dry this results in a hard dust-free surface so the paint will not soak in. Also the paint will be easier to apply.

Timber fences can be painted with normal gloss paint formulated for outdoor use. First use a priming paint on any untreated timber. Always apply an undercoat before the final gloss coat. I recommend gloss paint, for this is less inclined than matt-finish paints to attract dirt and grime.

MIRRORS

Why not consider mounting a large mirror on a wall? Like light-coloured paint, it will reflect light, although even more effectively. Also it will create the illusion of depth in the corner, as if the garden extends beyond the wall.

You will probably have to order a mirror specially for outdoor use as it should be made of heavy plate glass and must have a waterproof back. Also it should have pre-drilled holes so that you can fix it to the wall by means of brass screws (these must be buffered with special plastic or rubber washers). A suitable framework around the mirror will hide the screw heads.

A mirror must be framed in some way. I would suggest ordering a mirror with an arched top, which you could then frame with false-perspective trellis to give the impression of an arched path. Some garden centres supply false-perspective trellis units: generally they are painted white. An arched mirror could, alternatively, be surrounded with ordinary diamond-pattern trellis, again painted white.

Climbing plants can be grown up the trellis and the odd shoot should be allowed to hang down over the mirror so that its reflection will further help to create a sense of depth.

LIGHTING

Artificial lighting can be used in the corner at night, and also of course during the daytime if the corner is very dark and dingy. Spotlights can be used to illuminate plants (for example, a climber on the wall), a mirror or a piece of

statuary or other garden ornament. There are available both low-powered spotlights to illuminate small areas and stronger ones to light up larger areas.

Floodlights will, of course, almost provide a daylight effect and could be the answer to that very dark passageway between two houses, although do make sure that such powerful lighting does not annoy your neighbours.

A good garden centre or electrical shop should be able to supply both high-powered mains lighting systems and low-voltage systems. The latter are generally operated via a transformer which is kept indoors. One word of warning – it is absolutely vital that you use only outdoor lighting equipment in the garden, as this is completely waterproof.

STATUARY

Light-coloured statuary will also help to brighten a dark dingy corner. Choose white, off-white or cream-coloured pieces for maximum effect. If you cannot afford genuine stone statues, then go for those made from reconstituted stone. You will be hard-pressed to tell them apart from genuine stone statuary and they last for a great many years – at least a lifetime. Reconstituted stone is made from finely crushed stone mixed with cement; it is then formed into a dough-like consistency and pressed into moulds.

Concrete ornaments are cheaper and may not look so good at close range – an important consideration in a small corner.

Garden designers often set statuary in the corners of gardens so we are, therefore, following a well-tried practice. The size of the piece must, of course, be in scale with the garden: avoid an extremely large statue which would dominate the garden and, conversely, do not opt for a very tiny piece which would have no impact. Simply use your judgement.

There are various types of statue suitable for corners. Busts are popular mounted on plinths or on low walls (for example, the wall of a raised bed). Or you may wish to opt for a complete figure. A small figure could be mounted on a pedestal to give extra height.

This dramatic bust mounted on a pedestal is surrounded with hostas (plantain lilies) and astilbes with feathery plumes of flowers. It is backed by *Hedera colchica* (Persian ivy).

19

The use of plants around statuary is extremely important for they help to integrate it into the overall design. A statue in complete isolation looks rather 'lonely' and out on a limb. Firstly, ensure there is a suitable background of foliage. In our particular case this could be provided by climbing plants on the wall or fence. Have plenty of foliage plants around the base of a statue, too, or around the plinth or pedestal on which it stands, and allow them to partially cover the base. Examples of climbers and foliage plants for shade are described on p.10

CONSIDER THE GROUND

A further way of lightening a dark, gloomy corner is to surface the ground with a light-coloured material – again to help reflect light.

Light-coloured concrete paving slabs could be used, say, in shades of pale grey, pale stone colours or pastel green. These are easily laid on a firm foundation consisting of about 10 cm (4 in) of well-rammed hardcore topped with a 5 cm (2 in) layer of soft builders' sand. Each slab is laid on five spots of mortar, leaving narrow joints or gaps between each, which are later filled with mortar.

Slabs could be left out here and there for planting, or even complete beds could be incorporated into the paved area. In these areas omit the hardcore and fill with good quality topsoil.

Light-coloured gravel, such as pea shingle, which is available from builders' merchants, also makes a good surface and works out cheaper than paving slabs. It can simply be laid on well-firmed soil, but if you want a really hard surface, mix some dry cement into the soil before firming it. The cement will eventually harden and bind the soil together. Plants can be planted in a gravel area so take this into account when preparing the site (wherever plants are to be grown the soil will not need

firming and cement should certainly not be added to planting sites).

Very light-coloured cobbles or smooth pebbles, say in pale grey or buff, could be used for small areas, or combined with paving slabs or gravel in larger areas. Again, they should have a firm foundation and must be bedded in mortar.

HELPFUL HINTS

The problem with a gloomy corner, particularly if it is inclined to be damp, is that green moss and algae can build up on the walls and paving. These look unsightly, particularly with a painted wall, and they can make paving slippery, especially when the weather is wet.

Fortunately this green film can be removed, and quite easily if you catch it before it spreads too far, by treating the wall or paving with a proprietary masonry wash or horticultural algicide. Use these according to the maker's instructions and do not allow them to come into contact with plants as they can result in damage to foliage and stems.

After such treatment the moss or algae is easily removed with a scrubbing brush and plain water.

If you do not like moss or algae developing on statuary, this can be treated in the same way.

It probably goes without saying that the mirror should be kept scrupulously clean, otherwise the illusion will be spoiled. Simply wash it over as necessary with plain water.

If you have laid a gravel area and weeds start to grow up through it, treat it with a proprietary path weedkiller, according to the maker's directions.

CHAPTER TWO

BOGS AND DESERTS

Some people will no doubt have corners with extreme soil conditions, such as very wet ground or excessively dry soil. These lend themselves to being transformed into exciting and unusual features.

A MEDITERRANEAN CORNER

A little bit of rugged Mediterranean countryside is an excellent theme for a corner with very dry soil which is fully exposed to the sun.

———

A WOODLAND THEME

If the corner has dry soil with shade, consider a woodland theme, complete with appropriate stone ornaments.

———

POOL WITH ORNAMENTS AND BOG PLANTS

A corner with permanently wet soil makes a suitable site for a garden pool and an ideal home for unusual and bizarre bog plants.

BOGS

A
Mediterranean
Corner

AND DESERTS

If you have a corner with very dry soil which is fully exposed to the sun you have an ideal site for a little 'Mediterranean corner'.

Give it a rugged look to resemble Mediterranean countryside. You will need a few well-shaped specimen rocks to partially sink into the soil here and there. Then, after planting, the ground can be covered with rock fragments or stone chippings.

To help create the right atmosphere still further have some small terracotta urns scattered around among the plants – one or two can even be lying on their sides as though they have been accidentally knocked over.

Whether or not you have garden ornaments will depend on if you can find suitable subjects. What we really need in our Mediterranean corner is a stone lizard or snake draped over a rock, or even a tortoise nestling among the plants. Failing these, be content with your terracotta urns, which will also help create the right atmosphere.

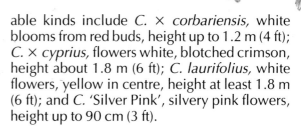

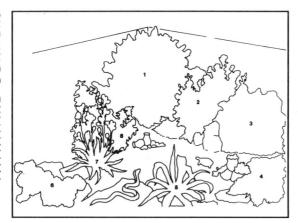

1. *Spartium junceum* (Spanish broom)
2. *Cistus* 'Silver Pink' (rock rose)
3. *Phlomis fruticosa*
4. *Genista lydia* (broom)
5. *Agave americana* 'Marginata' (century plant)
6. *Aeonium tabulaeforme* (saucer plant)
7. *Eryngium bromeliifolium*
8. *Cistus laurifolius* (rock rose)

A CHOICE OF PLANTS

The following plants will thrive in hot dry places and will help to create that Mediterranean atmosphere.

Anthemis cupaniana A dwarf spreading perennial with grey ferny foliage and a long succession of white daisy flowers in summer. Height up to 30 cm (12 in).

Centranthus ruber (red valerian) Herbaceous perennial with greyish green leaves and heads of dark pink or red flowers over a long period in summer. Height 45–90 cm (18–36 in).

Cistus (rock rose) Dwarfish bushy evergreen shrubs with flowers like single roses produced in spring and summer. There are lots of species and varieties, some hardier than others. Reli-

able kinds include *C.* × *corbariensis*, white blooms from red buds, height up to 1.2 m (4 ft); *C.* × *cyprius*, flowers white, blotched crimson, height about 1.8 m (6 ft); *C. laurifolius*, white flowers, yellow in centre, height at least 1.8 m (6 ft); and *C.* 'Silver Pink', silvery pink flowers, height up to 90 cm (3 ft).

Cytisus purgans (broom) This is a dwarf broom growing to about 1.2 m (4 ft) in height with a very bushy habit. In spring it is smothered with scented deep yellow flowers.

Eryngium Any of these herbaceous perennials are suitable for a hot dry spot but try some of the more unusual kinds, too, like *E. bromeliifolium* which forms a large rosette of long, tooth-edged leaves and heads of green flowers in summer; height up to 1.2 m (4 ft). A smaller but distinctive species is *E. variifolium* with rosettes of white-marbled leaves and heads of blue flowers in summer; height about 60 cm (2 ft).

Genista (broom) There are plenty of genistas for hot dry corners but dwarf kinds, suitable for the smaller garden, include *G. hispanica* (the Spanish gorse), a very dense prickly shrub with deep yellow flowers in summer, height about 1 m (3 ft); and *G. lydia*, an arching shrub about 60 cm (2 ft) in height with masses of brilliant yellow blooms in spring.

Morina longifolia This is a thistle-like herbaceous plant with very prickly foliage and spikes of white flowers, which later turn to purple, in the summer. Height at least 60 cm (2 ft).

Phlomis Small shrubs and herbaceous plants revelling in hot dry conditions. Try the Jerusalem sage, *P. fruticosa*, an evergreen shrub with grey hairy leaves and heads of yellow flowers in summer, height 1 m (3 ft); and *P. russeliana* (*P. viscosa*), a herbaceous perennial with big crinkly leaves and similar blooms, height up to 1.2 m (4 ft).

Phygelius capensis A perennial for mild areas only, with showy tubular red flowers throughout summer and into autumn. Height up to 1 m (3 ft).

Pinus (pine) Some of the dwarf pines can be recommended for our hot dry spot, including *P. leucodermis* 'Compact Gem', forming a deep green dome up to 1.8 m (6 ft) in height; *P. mugo* varieties, also dome-shaped and of similar height; and *P. sylvestris* 'Beuvronensis' which slowly makes a compact dome up to 1.8 m (6 ft) in height.

Spartium junceum (Spanish broom) This is a useful shrub for giving extra height to a planting scheme. It has thin green stems to a height of at least 2.4 m (8 ft) and throughout summer produces scented, deep yellow, pea-shaped flowers.

Zauschneria californica (Californian fuchsia) A shrubby, somewhat tender plant only recommended for mild areas. It's rather fuchsia-like in appearance, with red tubular flowers in late summer and autumn. Height up to 45 cm (18 in).

BULBS AND SUCCULENTS

There are numerous bulbs which can be used for drifting among these plants including allium (ornamental onion), colchicum (autumn crocus), crocuses of all kinds, ornithogalum (star of Bethlehem), scilla (squill) and dwarf tulip species. Mass plant these in bold groups and drifts.

Cacti and succulents, grown in pots, could be put outside for the summer, once danger of frost is over, and taken back inside in autumn before the frosts start again. These will further help to create a Mediterranean atmosphere. The pots could be plunged to their rims in soil among the permanent plants. One should certainly include the century plant, *Agave america,* and its variety 'Marginata' with yellow-edged leaves. They form rosettes of stiff, sword-like leaves each with a spine at the tip.

The succulent echeverias and aloes are also recommended, as is the very striking saucer plant, *Aeonium tabulaeforme,* from Tenerife, which produces a large rosette of leaves looking rather like a saucer, hence the common name. It is a monocarpic species – that is, it dies after flowering.

Cacti and succulents must be taken back indoors before the frosts start in the autumn. They should be overwintered in cool conditions, but placed in really bright light. Generally they do not need watering between mid-autumn and early spring as during this period they are resting. However, if plants start to shrivel unduly, then an application of water should be given – a thorough soaking.

HELPFUL HINTS

Even though the plants recommended here tolerate very dry conditions, it nevertheless pays to prepare the soil as well as possible before planting so that they subsequently make good growth, rather than remaining as small stunted specimens, as they often are in the wild where conditions may be very sparse.

In order to help conserve soil moisture, dig in plenty of bulky organic matter before planting, such as peat, pulverized bark, leafmould, spent hops, spent mushroom compost or garden compost.

During very dry weather in the spring and summer it is advisable to water the plants regularly as, again, growth will be very much better. Certainly young plants need watering until they are well established.

Another problem spot you may have is extremely dry soil with shade. This is often found under a tree, which takes most of the moisture out of the soil during the summer. It can also be experienced when a boundary hedge forms the corner; again this can cause the soil to dry out excessively, especially during spring and summer. In one of my previous gardens I had a boundary hedge of beech *(Fagus sylvatica)* forming a corner. In this corner was a mature laburnum or golden-rain tree and on the other side of the hedge, in my neighbour's garden, was a huge lilac (syringa). You can probably imagine what the soil was like in the height of the growing season – moisture was almost non-existent! The corner was also shaded by all of these plants, yet I managed to have a good plant display in this corner, using many of the subjects recommended below.

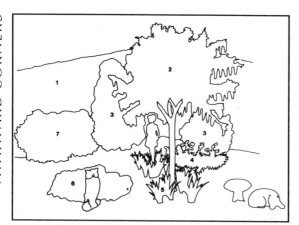

1. *Fagus sylvatica* (beech hedge)
2. Laburnum (golden rain)
3. Ilex (holly)
4. *Helleborus foetidus* (stinking hellebore)
5. *Iris foetidissima* (stinking iris)
6. *Geranium macrorrhizum* (crane's-bill)
7. *Skimmia reevesiana*

Before you attempt planting in these conditions it pays to prepare the soil thoroughly, which means digging in copious amounts of bulky organic matter like well-rotted farmyard manure, garden compost, peat or pulverized bark. Then after planting, ensure there is a permanent mulch of organic matter over the soil surface to help conserve moisture. This layer should be at least 5 cm (2 in) thick, using any of the materials recommended above. It goes without saying that applying water in the spring and summer will help plants to make steady growth.

As in other corners, appropriate statuary will help to create atmosphere. A woodland theme might be appropriate, especially if you have a hedge and/or a tree in the corner. Therefore try to find ornaments such as squirrels, doves, badgers, owls, a wood nymph (one of the youthful female divinities) and even a toadstool-shaped stone seat.

Light-coloured stone or reconstituted stone statuary would perhaps show up best in this corner, although one should not dismiss bronze (which is very expensive), bronze resin or lead ornaments, particularly if you can provide a light-coloured background for them, or the shade is not too heavy.

SUITABLE PLANTS

The following plants are extremely tolerant and should establish in this particular corner. It would pay to water them regularly after planting, until they are well established.

Arum italicum 'Pictum' A tuberous-rooted perennial with exotic white-veined spear-shaped leaves and sail-like flowers which are followed by heads of red berries. Height about 45 cm (18 in).

Two desirable woodland plants. *Arum italicum* 'Pictum' *(left)* has white-veined leaves and sail-like flowers; and *Liriope muscari (right)* bears spikes of mauve flowers in autumn.

Epimedium (barrenwort) Dwarf ground-covering herbaceous perennials with attractive foliage, often bronze-tinted, and dainty white, red or orange flowers in spring and early summer. Any of the many available species are suitable. Height around 30 cm (12 in).

Euphorbia (spurge) Several of these herbaceous perennials are suitable, including *E. cyparissias* of ground-covering habit with yellowish-green flowers in spring. It is rather invasive and grows to 30 cm (12 in) in height. *E. robbiae* also has yellowy green blooms, but in summer, and attains 45 cm (18 in) in height.

Geranium (crane's-bill) Herbaceous perennials of a ground-covering nature. Try *G. macrorrhizum* with aromatic foliage and pink flowers throughout summer (white in variety 'Album'), height at least 30 cm (12 in); and *G. phaeum* (the mourning widow) with deep purple flowers in early summer, 45 cm (18 in) high.

Helleborus foetidus (stinking hellebore) This evergreen perennial has attractive deep green glossy foliage and heads of yellowy green flowers in spring. Height 60 cm (2 ft).

Holcus mollis 'Variegatus' This is a dwarf grass, about 15 cm (6 in) high, with conspicuous white-edged leaves. It can be invasive although any surplus is easily forked out.

Ilex (holly) Any of the hollies are suitable and are useful evergreen shrubs for giving height to the planting scheme. They are slow growing. Choose any of the variegated varieties if you want to lighten the corner; for berries there is none finer than *I. aquifolium* 'J.C. van Tol' with almost spineless foliage.

Iris foetidissima (stinking iris, gladwyn iris) This has evergreen grassy foliage which gives off an unpleasant smell when crushed. Light purple flowers appear in early summer followed by striking red seeds. Height 60 cm (2 ft).

Liriope muscari Evergreen perennial with grassy foliage and spikes of mauve flower in late summer and autumn. Height about 30 cm (12 in).

Pachysandra terminalis Evergreen ground-cover plant with whorls of deep green foliage, white-edged in the variety 'Variegata'. Height about 30 cm (12 in).

Pulmonaria (lungwort) Dwarf ground-covering perennials flowering in spring. Several species, including *P. angustifolia* (blue flowers); *P. officinalis* (leaves spotted white, flowers purplish blue); and *P. saccharata* (white-spotted leaves, pink blooms changing to blue). Height 30 cm (12 in).

Skimmia reevesiana Compact, mound-like evergreen shrub with red berries throughout winter. Height about 60 cm (2 ft). There are several other skimmias that could be grown, too, but bear in mind with these that male and female flowers are carried on separate plants so you will need bushes of both sexes for berries to be produced. The varieties of *S. japonica* are recommended such as 'Foremanii', a female with large clusters of red berries; 'Fragrans', a male with lightly scented white blooms; 'Nymans', a female with large red berries, freely produced; and 'Rubella', a male noted for its trusses of red buds in winter which open into white flowers in spring. Another skimmia worth growing is *S. laureola* with red berries on female plants.

Symphytum grandiflorum (comfrey) A rough-leaved ground-cover perennial with tubular white blooms in spring. Very vigorous. Height up to 30 cm (12 in).

Waldsteinia ternata A charming carpeting perennial rather like a strawberry, but with conspicuous yellow blooms in spring. Height about 10 cm (4 in).

Pool With Ornaments & Bog Plants

In some corners the soil may remain permanently wet, particularly if it is a low-lying area into which rainwater drains. The theme here can be moisture or water, so a pool could be formed and bog plants grouped in the moist soil. Many ordinary garden plants will not thrive in such conditions, but there is certainly no shortage of exciting, unusual and even bizarre plants that relish moist ground.

I hope you will agree that this particular corner is both dramatic and exciting; and yet it is quite easily constructed and planted.

I should say at the outset that for this scheme you need a sunny corner, for bog plants, and aquatics grown in the pool, need plenty of sun if they are to grow well. A water and bog garden in complete shade will be a failure.

As in many other corners, appropriate statuary has been included to help create atmosphere.

1. *Gunnera manicata*
2. *Osmunda regalis* (royal fern)
3. *Lysichitum americanum* (skunk cabbage)
4. Rushes
5. *Scirpus tabernaemontani* 'Zebrinus' (zebra rush)

THE POOL

For this particular corner I would suggest a natural-looking pool, of informal shape, at or slightly below ground level. Water, overflowing from the pool, will further help to keep the surrounding soil wet. All kinds of bog or moisture-loving plants could be planted around the pool.

Today it is very easy to make a pool. The simplest method is to sink one of the prefabricated fibreglass pools into the ground and to hide the edges with flat pieces of natural stone. It is not much more difficult to make a pool from a butyl-rubber pool liner. The excavation is first lined with soft sand, the liner is loosely laid across the hole which is then filled with water, and the overlapping edges are again hidden with flat pieces of stone.

One delightful aspect of a pool is that it attracts a different range of wildlife, such as frogs, newts and dragonflies, and provides a watering place for birds, hedgehogs and other creatures. It may also attract herons, even in urban areas, if it is stocked with fish, but this is a problem rather than an asset, for a heron can clear a pool of fish for its breakfast!

Provided the ground stays wet it is not absolutely necessary to have a pool for the plants recommended later in this chapter, but it does make an enjoyable feature.

ORNAMENTS

Garden ornaments could certainly be used in the wet corner but you should choose appropriate kinds. For example, what could be more appropriate than stone frogs peering out of a group of rushes? Lead herons are extremely popular and would certainly look at home in this particular corner of the garden. To integrate the herons into the design, plant some groups of rushes around them.

If you want to include a human figure in this corner then try to choose something that looks as though it is involved with water – perhaps a nude or partly clothed figure that is contemplating bathing in the pool.

PLANTS FOR WET PLACES

As well as ordinary moisture-loving plants take the opportunity, if space permits, to grow some of the more unusual and bizarre bog plants which are guaranteed to amuse your visitors.

Cornus (shrubby dogwood) This is an ordinary but nevertheless highly colourful moisture-loving shrub at its most striking in winter when the brilliant red or yellow stems show up really well, especially when the sun shines on them. *Cornus alba* 'Sibirica', the Westonbirt dogwood, has brilliant crimson stems, while those of *C. stolonifera* 'Flaviramea' are bright yellow. If space permits, plant dogwoods in a bold group. The stems must be cut down almost to

ground level in mid-spring each year to ensure a good crop of young shoots which have the best colour. Height up to 2.4 m (8 ft). Can be grown in full sun or partial shade.

Gunnera manicata Not everyone will be able to grow this bizarre plant as it makes a massive specimen up to 3 m (10 ft) in height and spread. It is like a giant rhubarb, with prickly stems, and dies down to the ground each autumn. As it is not too hardy the crown of the plant should be covered in autumn with a few of its own leaves then further protected with a heap of straw, soil or peat. Remove in spring. Can be grown in sun or partial shade. The plant is so large that a person can easily stand under the leaves to shelter from the rain. It would be rather amusing to position a statue under it.

Iris There are several moisture-loving irises with attractive sword- or grass-like foliage and colourful blooms in summer. I can recommend the Japanese clematis-flowered iris, *I. kaempferi,* with exotic-looking blooms, and *I. sibirica,* both in a range of colours and growing to 1 m (3 ft) in height. They need full sun and *I. kaempferi* must have lime-free soil.

Juncus (bog rush) The rushes are essential plants for wet places. To say the least, *J. effusus* 'Spiralis' is a bizarre variety, with its curiously twisted, thin cylindrical leaves looking like corkscrews (it is popularly called the corkscrew rush). Height 45 cm (18 in). *J. glaucus* has ultra-thin grey leaves and grows up to 1 m (3 ft) in height. Both are evergreen and can be grown in sun or semi-shade.

Lysichitum americanum (skunk cabbage) This is another bizarre bog plant which never fails to result in gasps of amazement when it's in flower. This perennial is in the arum family and in spring produces bold yellow spathes up to 45 cm (18 in) in height. These are followed by large bright green leaves up to 1 m (3 ft) in length. The skunk cabbage is adaptable and can be grown in sun or semi-shade.

Osmunda regalis (royal fern) This is a tall stately fern up to 1.2 m (4 ft) in height, with medium green fronds which take on golden-brown tints in autumn before dying down for the winter. It can be grown in sun or semi-shade. When the stems have died back they should be cut down to the base.

Salix alba (willow) There are two varieties of this willow which are noted for their colourful stems in winter. They are grown in the same way as *Cornus* (see above) and must be pruned in the same way. They will also attain a similar height. *S. alba* 'Chermesina' (the scarlet willow) has bright orange-red stems while those of *S. alba* 'Vitellina' (the golden willow) are bright deep yellow.

Sambucus (elder) The elders will flourish in moist soils, including the *S. nigra* varieties 'Aurea' (yellow foliage), 'Albovariegata' (cream-edged leaves) and 'Aureomarginata' (yellow-edged leaves). Although fairly tall shrubs, they can be pruned back hard in mid-spring each year. Suitable for sun or semi-shade.

Scirpus tabernaemontani 'Zebrinus' (zebra rush). This is a striking rush for wet soil or shallow water, with its tall cylindrical leaves boldly banded with white and green. Herbaceous in habit, it is not too hardy and the crowns should be covered with peat or leafmould for the winter unless they are under water. This will keep them more compact and manageable. Height up 1 m (3 ft). Sun or partial shade. Another variety of *Scirpus tabernaemontani* is 'Albescens' (also known as *S. albescens).* It grows to a height of about 1.8 m (6 ft) and the stems are striped vertically with green and white. This is a popular variety with flower arrangers and hardier than 'Zebrinus'. It will grow either in shallow water or wet soil.

Zantedeschia aethiopica 'Crowborough' (arum lily) can be grown in shallow water or moist soil but is not too hardy. Suitable for sun or partial shade.

Zantedeschia aethiopica 'Crowborough' (arum lily) This herbaceous plant has attractive arrow-like foliage and white arum-like spathes in early summer. Height up to 1 m (3 ft). It can be grown in shallow water or in moist soil but is not too hardy. Unless in water, cover crown of plant for the winter with a mound of straw or leafmould. For sun or partial shade.

There are lots of other plants suitable for wet conditions, including astilbes, hostas (plantain lilies), bog primulas, *Filipendula ulmaria* (meadow sweet) and trollius (globe flowers). All are suitable for partial shade or sun.

HELPFUL HINTS

To the dismay of many people the water in a new pool turns green, like pea soup. But there is no need to worry about this for, if the pool is well planted, the water will gradually become clear again. On no account change the water, as it will simply turn green once more.

Submerged oxygenating plants will help to keep the water clear, so plant plenty of these. Many people call them water weeds. Popular and easily obtained kinds include the common fish weed *(Lagarosiphon major)*, Canadian pondweed *(Elodea canadensis)*, water violet *(Hottonia palustris)*, and the milfoils *(Myriophyllum spicatum* and *M. verticillatum)*. Bunches of these oxygenating plants are simply dropped into the water.

Water-lily pads will shade part of the pool and again help to ensure well-balanced conditions with crystal-clear water. No more than one-third of the water surface should be shaded by lily pads, though.

The clump-forming perennial plants for wet places such as juncus, lysichitum, scirpus, zantedeschia, astilbes, hostas, trollius, etc. may need lifting and dividing every four years or so, particularly if they are becoming congested. This is best carried out in mid-spring, just as they are starting to grow. Replant the young outer parts of each clump.

CHAPTER THREE

WEAR AND TEAR

Muddy patches where nothing grows indicate heavily used areas. With a little thought, such places can be turned into attractive features.

AROUND THE FRONT DOOR

How to create smart but durable areas around the front door – and not forgetting the back door and front gates.

――――

SMARTENING UP UTILITY CORNERS

Making a smart, permanent cupboard for all your tools, dustbins, etc., plus a decorative vegetable patch.

――――

THE CHILDREN'S CORNER

Creating an exciting, 'secret' play area for older children; and tips on keeping toddlers happy.

WEAR
Around The Front Door
AND TEAR

Muddy patches where nothing grows, except perhaps for some scruffy shrubs which were planted long ago but which have since been trodden on and generally mis-treated, indicate heavily used areas with frequent comings and goings. Where do we find these places? Most frequently around the front gate and around the front and back doors. Places, in fact, which particularly need to be kept smart to create the impression that you really do look after your garden! Smarten up these areas and you also ensure a pleasant welcome for your visitors.

1. Topiary specimens
2. Climbing rose
3. Heathers
4. *Juniperus horizontalis* variety (creeping juniper)
5. *Thymus serpyllum* (thyme)
6. Basket of summer bedding plants

The corner areas around the front gate and front and back doors, because they are used a great deal, need to be kept fairly simple in design and any plants used should be capable of withstanding the jostlings of children and general frantic comings and goings which seem to be part of modern living! Therefore it is unlikely that delicate, easily damaged plants like summer bedding and bulbs will stand a chance of creating the colourful display that they are capable of in other parts of the garden.

CHOOSING A SURFACE

The first consideration should be a durable surface to get rid of those mud patches. It is likely there is a patio or other hard-paved area outside the door, in which case we do not have a problem. But this is not always the case. Sometimes all one has is a path, no wider than the front gate or the house doors, and conse-

quently people are inclined to use the areas on each side of it in the vicinity of entrances. Hence the mud patches.

If you do not want to embark on extensive paving, then do at least widen the path on each side of the front gate and house doors. An area of at least double the width of a door or gate would not be too much, using the same material as the path.

Alternatively the material could be completely different to give a contrast in 'texture': gravel or cobbles, for instance, which have already been recommended on p. 20.

If you want a 'softer' effect then grass may be the answer – but not real grass as this would soon become threadbare and muddy. Rather, imitation or plastic grass which, today, is very well made and indeed often used in sports grounds. It should be laid on a firm surface and one way of achieving this is to mix dry cement into the soil surface and then to firm the ground really well. Eventually the cement will set, binding the soil together to create a really hard surface.

If you have quite an informal garden, perhaps a cottage-style which is very popular today with owners of town gardens, then consider surfacing the areas on each side of the gate or door with pulverized or chipped bark, choosing a grade specially recommended for surfacing. Bark creates a very soft surface and if the ground is prepared as described under artificial grass, you will have no problems of mud creeping up from below. Chipped bark can be laid about 5 cm (2 in) thick.

TOPIARY

What about plants on each side of the front or back door? Very fashionable today is the use of topiary specimens grown in tubs. There are several suppliers of topiary but I have to be honest and say that you need a fairly deep pocket to buy 'ready made' topiary. However,

a pair of topiary specimens placed each side of a door does create a sophisticated atmosphere.

Topiary is normally formed of box, *Buxus sempervirens,* an evergreen shrub with small deep green foliage. It is formed into various shapes by the 'trainers', such as a tall corkscrew shape, and looks superb in square wooden tubs painted white.

Sweet bay, *Laurus nobilis,* is also used and often formed into a round-headed tree with a bare trunk (this style of plant is very fashionable) or into a cone shape. The sweet bay is also an evergreen shrub, but with larger leaves than box. The highly aromatic leaves are used in cooking for flavouring, so a bay tree outside the kitchen door would be both practical and decorative.

These topiary specimens are quite tough and will survive in the areas we are considering, but bear in mind that bay is not one of the hardiest plants and should be given a position well sheltered from cold winds. It is a better choice for milder southern parts of the country than very cold northern areas. However, in less-favoured areas it could perhaps be overwintered in a frost-free greenhouse or conservatory.

To keep your topiary specimens looking neat they need to be clipped regularly with shears (secateurs for bay) in the spring and summer, as considered necessary.

TOUGH SPREADERS

Tough low-growing plants which could be planted on each side of the widened path to 'soften' the edges include the prostrate junipers such as *Juniperus horizontalis* varieties with well-textured evergreen foliage in many shades of green, 'blue' or grey. Junipers don't mind being trodden on occasionally! The same applies to creeping thymes, varieties of *Thymus serpyllum,* and indeed bruising of the foliage releases their pleasant aromatic fra-

rance. Heathers, once established, will tolerate a stray foot now and again. Particularly attractive are the golden-foliage varieties of the ling, *Calluna vulgaris,* which are colourful all the year round, and the varieties of *Erica herbacea (E. carnea)* which produce carpets of pink, red or white flowers in the winter and early spring.

If real plants do not stand a chance in these areas, then why not resort to artificial kinds, such as a tubful of variegated plastic ivy and hydrangea, even if only for temporary display in the summer?

A GUIDING LIGHT

A welcome could be provided for visitors by installing an old-fashioned lamp-post near the front gate or front door. There is quite a demand these days for old gas lamps, which are easily converted to electricity. The lamp-post should be painted a pleasing colour – perhaps to match the house.

If you are an artist why not paint an ivy or some other climber growing up the lamp-post? Alternatively, train a real variegated ivy up it, but bear in mind that the ivy will have to be pruned regularly to prevent it from completely hiding the lamp-post.

If the lamp-post has a horizontal bar at the top (presumably used originally to support a ladder) you have the perfect support for a hanging basket.

Trailing summer bedding plants could then be grown in the basket as these provide plenty of colour over a long period – from early summer until well into autumn. Highly recommended for baskets are the pendulous varieties of greenhouse fuchsia. Also very popular are trailing or ivy-leaved pelargo-niums. Try the new Swiss balcony varieties as they are extremely free flowering. Other good basket plants are small flowered petunias, trailing lobelia, impatiens and white alyssum. 39

Smartening Up Utility Corners

Dustbins, odd tools, the lawnmower, etc, have to go somewhere and are generally relegated to an odd corner but there is no reason why they should be in full view, detracting from the pleasantness of the rest of the garden. Why not consider building a special but decorative cupboard for these items?

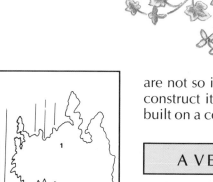

1. Variegated hedera (ivy)
2. Chimney pots filled with summer bedding plants
3. Troughs and tubs filled with summer bedding plants

A permanent cupboard of the height and size required could be built with ornamental concrete walling blocks which resemble natural stone. Incorporate timber doors in the front for access, painted to match the house, of course. I would suggest a flat roof as this is easy to construct and can be used as a display area for colourful plants. The roof can be boarded with timber and then weather-proofed with roofing felt, which is then covered with bitumen or tar, followed immediately by a layer of pea shingle.

Wooden troughs or window boxes could be placed on the roof around the edges, and filled with bedding plants for colour in spring and summer. Include some trailing kinds, such as lobelia, petunias and pendulous fuchsias, to cascade down the sides of the cupboard, so 'softening' the hard lines. Or use permanent trailers like variegated ivies. There might be room behind the troughs or window boxes for more plant containers.

The DIY enthusiast should be able to build a utility/dustbin cupboard quite easily, but if you are not so inclined then get a local builder to construct it for you. Remember that it is best built on a concrete base.

A VEGETABLE CORNER

A vegetable patch is, of course, a utility area and is often sited in a corner of the garden. However, there is no reason why it should constitute an eyesore. With a little thought and planning, it can be made into quite an attractive feature, which I feel is particularly important in a small garden.

The drawing shows an imaginative vegetable 'patch' in the corner of a small garden. The beds have been laid out in a geometric pattern with gravel paths between them. Each bed is devoted to a different kind of vegetable.

The aim has been to choose vegetables which are attractive and even highly colourful. However, they are not simply ornamental but very useful and delicious kinds.

In the centre bed there are dwarf bush tomatoes which produce large crops of small red fruits in the summer. Bush tomatoes do not need staking.

Instead of growing ordinary lettuce, why not try the cut-leaved, red-flushed variety 'Red Salad Bowl'. The leaves are picked individually throughout summer and make a colourful addition to any salad.

A rather unusual but delicious vegetable is the leaf beet ruby chard, with bright red stems which are cut up and boiled. The leaves are used as spinach. The asparagus pea is another unusual but delicious vegetable for summer use. The winged pods are picked when young and cooked whole. This low-spreading plant has attractive deep red flowers and indeed makes quite a colourful show.

Another suggestion is to grow beetroots, which have quite colourful reddish-purple stems and foliage.

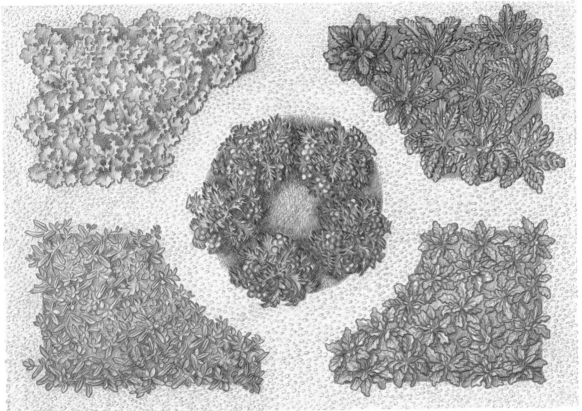

An imaginative vegetable 'patch'. The centre bed has bush tomatoes. *Top left:* lettuce 'Red Salad Bowl'. *Top right:* leaf beet ruby chard. *Bottom left:* asparagus peas. *Bottom right:* beetroots.

A SHADY SITE

Most vegetables require a corner which receives plenty of sun, otherwise growth and cropping will be poor. However, I realize that perhaps the only place some people have for growing vegetables is in a shady corner. Nevertheless, there are a few vegetables which can be grown in shade, provided the site is not overhung by trees, but rather is open to the sky and shaded by hedges, buildings, etc.

If the vegetable plot is in shade, then make best use of the late spring and summer months when the light is good, and grow beetroots, spring onions, kohl rabi and lettuce (especially small compact varieties). You should also be successful with summer and autumn cabbage.

Mint will thrive in shade but some people may find this too vigorous and spreading for a small garden. However, it can be controlled by planting it in a bottomless bucket sunk to its rim in the ground. This will certainly prevent the mint from spreading and swamping other plants.

Parsley is a popular herb and will also thrive in shade; as will the Hamburg parsley, a vegetable for winter use with celery flavoured parsnip-like roots.

43

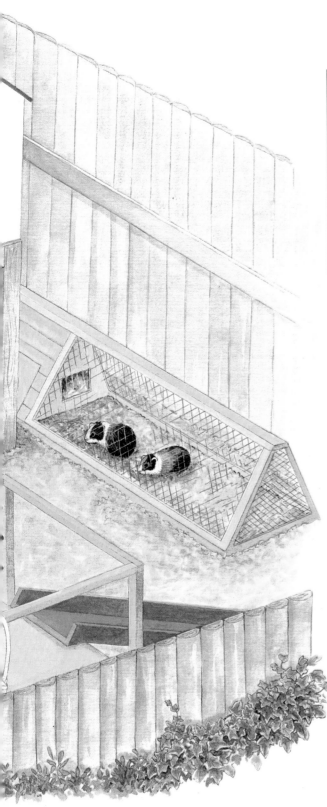

The Children's Corner

Children playing constantly in one part of the garden can, with all due respect to them, turn it into an eyesore. What with digging holes in the ground and general trampling, turning the ground into mud, a play area is not often a thing of beauty. Yet children should certainly not be discouraged from such activities – indeed, it is sensible to provide a special corner for them, so ensuring the rest of the garden remains unscathed.

SCREENING A CORNER

For older children, who do not require supervision from parents, I would suggest screening off a corner in some way. This not only provides a more exciting 'secret' play area for them, but also hides it from view. A strong screen about 1.8 m (6 ft) high is suggested.

A rather attractive screen can be formed with a palisade of logs or stout timber poles. These are inserted vertically well into the ground and they should butt hard up against each other. Horizontal timber rails should be nailed behind to hold them all together: two to three rails for a really secure job.

A much quicker and easier way of screening   **45**

1. Elevated cabin or play-house
2. Wire run for pets
3. Climbing frame and slide
4. Pet's hutch

a play area is to use prefabricated fencing panels of lapped or woven timber. But bear in mind that the timber is quite thin and a hard knock could result in a panel being damaged.

SPECIAL FEATURES

Consider a suitable surface for children to play on. It needs to be soft, particularly in the area of play equipment such as climbing frame, slide and see-saw. Pulverized or chipped bark is ideal, as discussed on p. 38. If a harder area is needed then consider installing timber decking which ensures a comparatively dry and certainly mud-free area in wet weather. This can be bought ready-made.

It is a good idea to provide some form of shelter, particularly for play during wet weather. The simplest can consist of a tarpaulin supported on a simple wooden framework. A cabin of some kind, such as a small log cabin, hardly ever fails to stimulate a sense of adventure in children. Cabins can be bought ready made, specially for children, or

the DIY enthusiast could perhaps build one reasonably inexpensively using secondhand timber. An elevated cabin, built on stout timber stilts, could be even more exciting for children and is the modern equivalent of a tree house.

If your children keep pets, like rabbits and guinea pigs, these could also be housed in this corner. I am in favour of having wire-netting runs as well as the normal hutches so that the animals get plenty of exercise. Remember, though, that pets should not be left unattended in open-topped runs, otherwise they could be attacked by foxes or cats.

What do you do with this screened corner when the children have grown up and no longer require it? The answer is to simply leave it intact, but of course clear out the play equipment – it will make a perfect utility corner for dustbins, compost heap, etc. If there is a cabin you might wish to retain this for use as a tool shed.

TODDLERS' CORNERS

What about tiny children who need constant parental supervision? They should have a play area next to the house where parents can easily keep an eye on them. Many parents provide a sand pit which can simply be a square or circular hole at least 30 cm (12 in) deep filled with clean soft sand. Make a timber cover for it to keep out cats when the sand pit is not in use and to keep the sand dry during wet weather.

When children no longer need a sand pit it could be turned into an ornamental pool, by making it a bit deeper – at least 45 cm (18 in) – and lining it with a butyl-rubber pool liner. Do bear in mind, though, that a pool can be a great danger to young children so don't be in too much of a rush – better to wait until your children are a bit older. In the meantime hide the timber cover using ornamental containers filled with colourful plants.

46

CHAPTER FOUR

COLOUR FOR ODD SPOTS

Colour is often lacking in corners and other odd parts of the garden. This can be remedied by using colourful objects and landscaping materials, in conjunction with suitable plants.

BRIGHTENING UP UGLY WALLS

Here we decorate a wall with trailing plants in wall pots, plaques and masks, and even with a mural.

CASCADES FOR STEEP BANKS

A bank often lacks colour and interest, but not if you construct a dramatic water cascade, and have drifts of colourful plants flowing down it.

CONTINUING COLOUR

A coloured pergola is the 'in thing' and ensures your garden is always attractive. Planting to ensure a succession of flower colour is also catching on.

AN ORIENTAL CORNER

Here we arrange coloured oriental figures and lanterns among Chinese and Japanese plants.

NARROW BEDS AND BORDERS

These can be difficult to plant effectively and often end up lacking depth and colour. Ideas on how to create the illusion of extra depth, and a choice of small plants to provide colour over a long period.

BRIGHTENING UP A DULL CONCRETE CORNER

Transforming an area of concrete by using brightly coloured containers and even coloured gravels.

Brightening Up Ugly Walls

FOR ODD SPOTS

Colour is often lacking in corners and other odd parts of the garden. Usually this is because the plants chosen do not provide continuous colour: after flowering they remain dull and uninteresting for many months. It is possible for a planting scheme to provide colour and interest all the year round if some thought is put into choosing plants. In most schemes there should be plants for each season of the year.

Furthermore it is not necessary to rely on plants alone: there are plenty of attractive materials and objects that could be combined with them to provide permanent colour, as shown in the drawings in this chapter. The idea of using colourful landscaping and construction materials in gardens is gradually becoming accepted by garden designers, but in some quarters it is still considered rather trendy or quirky.

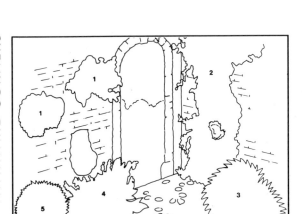

1. Wall pots filled with trailing bedding plants
2. Hedera (ivy)
3. Ornamental grasses
4. Hostas (plantain lilies)
5. Ornamental grasses

WALL ORNAMENTS

Apart from using colourful climbers, a good way of brightening up an ugly wall is to fix wall pots to it and fill them with suitable plants, such as those kinds used for hanging baskets (see p. 60). These containers are half-round ornamental pots which are screwed directly to walls. Many are made from warm orangy terracotta and are therefore attractive in themselves.

Wall plaques and masks can often provide a touch of humour, if not colour (although there are available colourful ceramic plaques). For instance, a grotesque mask or a joker peering out of a curtain of ivy often results in a chuckle from visitors. Wall plaques and masks are available in various materials such as terracotta, reconstituted stone and ceramic.

Another idea is to rummage around antique shops for old ceramic patterned tiles and to use 50 these like plaques. Often very colourful and

decorative, they will very much help to brighten up a drab wall.

A gargoyle or mask incorporating a water spout (such as the ever-popular lion mask) is another idea for a dull wall. They are mounted on the wall and some have a small self-contained dish to catch the water. Or the water can be allowed to fall into a small pool below. A small pump is used to circulate the water, which quickly evaporates in hot weather so it must be regularly topped up.

If there is a particularly attractive view beyond the wall why not consider making an opening in it so that you catch a glimpse of the scene from within your garden – say a circular or square 'window'? I would advise employing a builder to make a window in an existing wall for the edges of the opening will need reinforcing, perhaps with new brickwork. Then get a local blacksmith to make up an ornamental wrought-iron grid to fit the opening. This can be painted either black or white.

A MURAL

Another idea is to paint a mural on part or all of the wall: say a country or garden scene. Of course, you have to be quite a proficient artist to produce a realistic mural – a very deep pocket would be needed to commission a professional artist.

The area to be painted must be rendered with mortar to give a smooth flat surface and again this is a skilled job, best undertaken by a builder or plasterer. If the wall is already rendered, do make sure that the rendering is perfectly sound and not liable to fall away at a later date.

The wall must be dry internally – in other words, there must be no rising damp. All should be well if the wall is part of the house or garage as it should then have a damp-proof course.

The wall should be prepared for painting by

first treating it with a masonry type of stabilizing solution followed, when dry, with a coat or two of white masonry paint (it is best not to use the type which contains fine sand as this results in a somewhat sandpaper-like surface).

Artists' acrylic paints are used for murals, being quick-drying and waterproof. The completed mural should be sealed with two coats of artists' acrylic varnish.

A mural should be framed in some way, otherwise it will look like a picture 'hanging' on the wall. The aim should be to give the impression of a view as seen through a gap in the wall. The simplest way would be to paint a 'stone' or 'brick' arch around the mural.

The rest of the wall can then be painted with masonry paint if you wish to improve its appearance: perhaps a cheerful warm terracotta colour. Add a further touch of elegance by fixing some white-painted timber trellis panels to the wall on which to grow climbing plants.

Don't forget that a mural can also be enjoyed at night by using garden lighting to spotlight it. Indeed, the effect can be more dramatic than during the daytime.

I think that a mural should be in keeping with the garden and the surroundings. An exotic scene is not quite the thing for a western city or town garden, though I do know of such instances (for example, in a London garden there is a splendid mural depicting the Taj Mahal!).

I would suggest a garden scene in the same style as the real garden, perhaps a central path leading to a focal point with flower borders on either side, containing colourful summer flowering plants, and maybe a small tree or two.

Of course, if you live in the country, then a pleasant rural scene would be appropriate – perhaps a view of rolling downland and a group of trees. Include a good expanse of sky with white clouds.

HELPFUL HINTS

In this corner I have suggested that the ground is covered with cobbles. Large, round, smooth pebbles, such as beach pebbles, give an excellent cobbled effect and they are easily laid by bedding them close together in mortar.

It is also possible to buy paving stones in cobble effect and, of course, these are even easier to lay, again on spots of mortar.

You will notice that I have left planting areas for such plants as hostas or plantain lilies and ornamental grasses, which further help to give character to this corner.

One point to bear in mind about plants in wall pots is that they can rapidly dry out in warm weather, just like hanging baskets, and so one should keep a constant eye on them for water requirements. During hot weather they should be inspected twice a day as it is possible they will need watering in the morning and possibly again in the afternoon or evening. Many of these wall pots are porous and therefore moisture is lost all too quickly through the sides.

When the plants are established in wall pots they will need feeding regularly in the summer. A weekly or fortnightly liquid feed, using a proprietary flower-garden fertilizer, will help them to achieve optimum growth and flowering. Bedding plants that are used in wall pots should also have their dead flowers removed regularly, as this encourages continuous flowering.

Cascades For Steep Banks

I have come across numerous gardens which have steep banks in them and sadly the majority lack colour and interest. The problem is that many people do not really know what to do with a bank and generally resort to grassing it – with deadly dull results!

1. *Parthenocissus quinquefolia* (Virginia creeper)
2. *Campanula portenschlagiana* (bellflower)
3. *Cerastium biebersteinii* (snow-in-summer)

A WATER CASCADE

A popular feature for a bank is a natural-looking waterfall cascading into a pool below, perhaps in conjunction with a rock garden. This is a traditional feature and also quite expensive to construct. A more trendy idea for a modern town garden is a water cascade built of timber, zig-zagging down the bank into a formal pool at the bottom.

The DIY enthusiast should be able to construct these wooden 'troughs' easily enough and, to make them waterproof, they should be carefully lined with black butyl-rubber pool liner, securing it with a suitable bituminous adhesive. The pool excavation can also be lined with butyl rubber. An electric pump of suitable capacity is used to circulate the water from the pool to the top of the cascade.

Finally the outside parts of the cascade could be painted (perhaps black), or treated with a coloured wood preservative, such as red cedar or dark oak. This feature could be made very

attractive at night by illuminating it with coloured garden lights.

PLANT CASCADES

An attractive way of planting a bank is to have cascades of colourful plants flowing down it. This idea could be used in conjunction with a water cascade, or alone if desired.

Each subject used is mass planted in a bold drift to resemble a river winding its way down the bank. Plants with a spreading or carpet-forming habit are the best ones to use and, of course, they should be low-growing.

If you want to create a blue 'river' then choose one of the dwarf campanulas or bellflowers like *Campanula portenschlagiana* with blue bell-shaped flowers throughout summer and into autumn; or *C. poscharskyana* with light blue starry blooms over the same period. Plant about 60 cm (2 ft) apart each way. They tolerate partial shade. Another blue 'river' could be formed with a spring-flowering gentian, *Gentiana verna* 'Angulosa', with brilliant blue star-shaped flowers. Provide a position in sun and plant 15 cm (6 in) apart.

For a silver cascade there is the rather rampant *Cerastium bierbersteinii,* or snow-in-summer, with mats of evergreen silver-grey foliage and white flowers in spring and summer. Plant 60 cm (2 ft) apart and provide a sunny or partially shady position.

For a yellow effect I can recommend one of the mat-forming thymes: *Thymus* 'Anderson's Gold' with bright yellow foliage all the year round. Provide a position in sun and plant about 45 cm (18 in) apart. Or try the yellow-leaved lamb's ears, *Stachys olympica* 'Primrose Heron'. This evergreen perennial has golden felted leaves in the spring, which gradually change to a pale silver grey. Choose a position in sun or partial shade and plant about 30 cm (12 in) apart each way.

In the autumn the Virginia creeper, *Parth-*

enocissus quinquefolia, will create an effect like a flow of molten lava when its leaves turn vivid crimson. Although it is really a climber it can be used as ground cover, when it should be planted about 1.2 m (4 ft) apart each way. It is suitable for sun or partial shade.

The new ground-cover roses also lend themselves to planting in cascades and they produce masses of flowers in the summer. For a small bank one should choose those of medium vigour and plant them 60–90 cm (2–3 ft) apart each way, in full sun.

Try any of the following varieties: 'Ferdy', with an arching habit and small soft pink double flowers; 'Fiona', also with an arching habit, and semi-double deep red flowers; 'Nozomi', with a prostrate habit and small single flowers in very pale pink; 'Pink Bells', with an arching habit and double pale pink blooms; 'Pink Drift', a prostrate variety with small double pale pink flowers; 'Red Bells', an arching plant with brilliant crimson-red double flowers; 'Swany', prostrate habit, small double white flowers; 'The Fairy', bushy habit and small double pink blooms; and 'White Bells', an arching plant with white double flowers.

You will probably have to buy ground-cover roses from a rose specialist, although some garden centres are now stocking a limited selection.

Ground-cover roses will grow well in any soil, including dry sandy types. These are very resistant to the common rose diseases. No pruning needed.

A GROTTO

If you want a somewhat bizarre feature for part of a bank consider building a traditional grotto. A grotto is a small picturesque cave forming an attractive retreat, although I am not suggesting anything large enough to actually sit in!

Gardeners have been making grottoes since ancient times and they were particularly popular with the Victorians, who often decorated them inside by sticking shells, colourful rocks, stones and crystals, coloured glass, etc, to the walls. A modern addition would be to illuminate the inside at night with a coloured outdoor spotlight. A further embellishment would be to incorporate a small self-contained water feature in the grotto, such as a combined bowl and fountain.

To make a grotto you first dig a semi-circular hole in the base of the bank. Then you have to build an internal wall of some kind. For instance, you could use natural rock, bonding the pieces together with mortar. A more formal effect would be created with bricks or ornamental walling blocks. You could use inexpensive bricks and then render the walls with mortar to give a smooth finish. Any favourite objects like shells, coloured stones, glass, etc, could be pressed into the mortar as rendering proceeds.

Finally you will have to install a roof. There are various ways of doing this, like laying a large flat thick piece of rock or thick pieces of timber over the excavation, making sure they rest on the walls, of course. When designing a grotto bear in mind that the roof should be higher at the front than at the back so that you can easily see inside.

Trailing plants such as ivies could be used to cover the roof of the grotto, particularly if timber is used, which may not look very attractive by itself.

Continuing Colour

FOR ODD SPOTS

When certain plants have finished flowering, such as spring- or early summer-flowering shrubs and roses, a bed or border may be devoid of colour for the rest of the year. Therefore we need to combine with them other plants which will ensure continuing colour; and also consider the use of coloured woodwork.

1. Climbing roses
2. Forsythia
3. *Clematis viticella*

A HOST FOR CLEMATIS

A good way to ensure continuing colour from large shrubs, particularly spring- and early-summer flowering kinds, is to allow a summer- or autumn-flowering clematis to grow through them. Most clematis are slim climbers and provided they are not excessively vigorous will not actually swamp or dominate their host. (It should be said, though, that a clematis twining through a shrub does make the pruning of that shrub slightly more difficult and time-consuming.)

Clematis viticella is a good species to choose, especially as it is best pruned back to within 60 cm (2 ft) of the ground in late winter or early spring. Its blue or purplish bell-shaped flowers are produced from mid-summer to early autumn. There are several varieties of this species which are also recommended, like the deep purple 'Royal Velours', the lighter purple 'Abundance' and the white 'Alba Luxurians'.

Or you may wish to grow the large-flowered hybrid clematis, like the bright purple 'Jackma-

nii Superba', crimson-striped 'Nellie Moser' or the pale blue 'Mrs Cholmondeley'.

A COLOURED PERGOLA

One should also consider introducing colour by other means, rather than relying on plants alone. There is a trend towards coloured woodwork in gardens which makes a refreshing change from the normal timber colours like red cedar and dark oak. A pergola, for instance, could be painted. Why not try black uprights, with the cross pieces at the top painted red? A very smart combination and an ideal support for red climbing roses.

A pergola painted white can also look very smart, especially when it supports pink or red climbing roses, and perhaps a blue wisteria for spring colour.

UNDERPLANTING ROSES

Roses, of course, particularly the bedding kinds like the large-flowered (hybrid tea) and cluster-flowered (floribunda) varieties, have a long flowering season, from early summer through to the autumn. But for the rest of the year a rose bed is decidedly dull unless one uses other plants to extend the period of colour.

Roses can be underplanted with various low-growing plants. Colour will certainly be needed in the spring and what better than a collection of miniature bulbs. These can be drifted among the rose bushes or used as an edging for the bed. With blue flowers are the scillas, chionodoxas and muscari or grape hyacinths. Miniature bulbous irises also have blue flowers, as well as purple and yellow. Try small crocuses, too, like the *C. chrysanthus* varieties with flowers in shades of yellow, cream and blue. Use temporary spring bedding plants, like blue forget-me-nots or myosotis, and multicoloured polyanthus. Winter-

flowering pansies, such as the popular 'Universal' mixture, bloom throughout winter and into spring.

Also flowering in spring are several very popular perennials like aubrieta with mats of greyish foliage and flowers in shades of purple, blue, pink and red, and the yellow-flowered, grey-leaved *Alyssum saxatile*.

Providing foliage interest all year round, but particularly welcome in winter, is *Cerastium tomentosum,* or snow-in-summer, with silvery foliage and white flowers in summer; and *Stachys lanata* 'Silver Carpet', or lamb's ears, also with attractive silvery leaves. The ajugas or bugles are evergreen ground-cover plants grown mainly for their foliage, although they produce spikes of generally blue flowers in the spring. Choose *A. reptans* varieties like the purple-leaved 'Atropurpurea', the wine-red 'Burgundy Glow' and the cream and green variegated 'Variegata'.

Also making attractive evergreen ground cover are varieties of the common sage, *Salvia officinalis*. 'Purpurascens' has purple foliage, 'Icterina' is green and gold and 'Tricolor' has grey-green and white leaves flushed with purple and pink.

A really superb hardy perennial for growing among roses is nepeta (catmint). The best one to plant is *Nepeta ×faassenii,* which is often used for edging rose beds. It forms a bush covered with small, grey-green foliage and is highly aromatic. Between late spring and early autumn the plant bears spikes of light blue flowers. It grows to a height of 30 cm (1 ft) but the variety 'Six Hills Giant' is taller, up to 60 cm (2 ft). This one may well be a bit too tall for some rose beds.

The Christmas rose, *Helleborus niger,* will give interest in the winter with its white saucer-shaped flowers. Sometimes these are actually in bloom at Christmas time. The best variety to grow is 'Potter's Wheel' with extra-large flowers. Also try the winter-flowering iris, *Iris unguicularis,* with pale blue flowers amidst attractive grassy foliage. Also with grassy leaves is *Liriope muscari* which has spikes of blue flowers in autumn.

HELPFUL HINTS

Of course, when underplanting roses in this way feeding of the bushes becomes more difficult. And roses certainly need regular feeding – an application of proprietary rose fertilizer in the spring, and another after the first flush of blooms, in early summer. You will have to carefully work the fertilizer around each rose bush and lightly prick it into the soil surface with a hand fork. It is best not to allow the ground-covering plants to actually grow right up to the stems of the roses, but rather leave an area of bare soil around each bush.

Some of the hardy perennials which are recommended for rose beds, particularly cerastium, stachys, ajuga and liriope, should be lifted and divided about every three or four years in the early spring, to keep them young and vigorous. Simply lift them with a garden fork, shake off most of the soil, and pull them apart into hand-sized portions for replanting. Discard the centre part of each plant as this will be declining in vigour. Use only the young outer portions of each clump for replanting.

The other plants can be left alone, although groups of bulbs may need lifting, separating and replanting when they become congested and this is best done when their foliage has died down and they are resting.

59

An Oriental Corner

There are not many coloured garden
ornaments which can be used among
plants but there is a range of red oriental
stone figures and lanterns. With these
one could create an oriental corner,
using Chinese or Japanese plants, like
the Chinese witch hazel, *Hamamelis
mollis*, a deciduous slow-growing shrub
valued for its spidery yellow winter
flowers. Try to obtain the variety
'Pallida' with large light yellow blooms.

1. *Salix matsudana* 'Tortuosa' (twisted willow)
2. *Hamamelis mollis* (witch hazel)
3. *Nandina domestica* (Chinese sacred bamboo)
4. Dwarf evergreen azaleas

HELPFUL HINTS

Some of these plants, including the hamamelis, evergreen azaleas, nandina, paeonia and acer, like a moisture-retentive soil and a good way to help achieve this is to mulch the surface of the ground around the plants with organic matter. A 5 cm (2 in) layer of peat or pulverized bark can be recommended. Make sure the soil is moist before spreading the mulch and if necessary top it up in the spring. Pulverized bark is longer-lasting than peat and so will need topping up less often.

NARROW BEDS

If you want a small tree I suggest the Yoshino cherry, *Prunus × yedoensis,* which has a graceful arching habit and scented white blossoms in the early spring. A rather bizarre Chinese willow would look good in this corner: *Salix matsudana* 'Tortuosa' with curiously twisted stems and shoots. This shows up particularly well in the winter when the leaves have fallen.

For colour in spring or early summer plant a group of dwarf evergreen azaleas, provided you have acid or lime-free soil. There are lots of varieties including pink 'Hinomayo' and brilliant crimson 'Hinodegiri'. *Nandina domestica,* the Chinese sacred bamboo, is an unusual evergreen shrub needing a sheltered spot. The young leaves are tinted with red and in autumn become flushed with purple. Include the Chinese tree peony, *Paeonia lutea ludlowii,* with large yellow bowl-shaped flowers in early summer, and for brilliant autumn leaf colour a variety of *Acer palmatum,* or maple.

Very narrow beds and borders can be difficult to plant effectively and they often end up lacking depth. So why not try to create the illusion of extra depth by backing the border with a mirror? Ideally, of course, it should be the full length of the bed or border and at least the height of the plants used. Mirrors have been discussed on p.18. The mirror will reflect the plants and give the impression that the border is twice the width.

If you are an artist, and the border is backed by a suitable wall, you may wish instead to have a mural as a background (see p. 50). Ideally the mural should depict border plants, especially some taller kinds to give height to this feature. Then a collection of smaller plants could be planted in front of it.

HARDY PERENNIALS

In a very narrow bed or border you will have to choose small plants and there is certainly plenty of attractive kinds among the hardy

perennials. If the border is shaded then you could create an attractive scheme with small hostas or plantain lilies like *H. decorata, H. 'Ginko Craig'* and *H. tardiana*. All are superb foliage plants although they do produce spikes of lily-like flowers in summer. Combine these with candelabra primulas such as *Primula japonica* and its varieties which flower in summer, and the spring-flowering drumstick primrose, *P. denticulata*. Many of the hardy ferns would also be suitable for this scheme. For winter and spring flowers plant some groups of Lenten roses, *Helleborus orientalis*, with bowl-shaped blooms in various colours, from white to purple.

Requiring a sunny situation are small border plants like dwarf Michaelmas daisies which produce a bright splash of colour in autumn and grow no more than 30–45 cm (12–18 in) in height. Also flowering in autumn is *Sedum spectabile* with large flat heads of pink flowers. For summer colour there are small perennials like the bellflower, *Campanula carpatica*, with large blue bell-shaped flowers; border pinks or dianthus; *Liatris spicata* with spikes of pink flowers; and an evening primrose, *Oenothera missouriensis*, with large saucer-like pale yellow flowers. Dwarf irises could be included for early summer colour, and for foliage effect the small phormiums or New Zealand flaxes, with sword-like leaves, such as 'Yellow Wave' whose leaves are striped with golden-yellow and green.

SMALL SHRUBS

Small compact shrubs which could be combined with these perennials include *Choisya ternata* 'Sundance', an evergreen with the most brilliant golden foliage. It will grow well in sun or partial shade. Or how about a dwarf holly with golden foliage – *Ilex crenata* 'Golden Gem'? It has tiny leaves and is most

Narrow border backed by mirror. The plants are, from left to right: *Sedum spectabile* (butterfly plant), *Choisya ternata* 'Sundance', *Ruta graveolens* 'Jackman's Blue' (blue rue), and *Liatris spicata*.

un-holly-like, but a superb little shrub, best grown in a sunny spot. A really stunning shrub for acid or lime-free soil is *Leucothoe fontanesiana* 'Rainbow' whose new foliage, in early summer, is splashed with cream, yellow and pink. It will be happy in full sun or partial shade and can be pruned after flowering (it produces white blooms) to keep it really compact.

The blue rue, *Ruta graveolens* 'Jackman's Blue', has pungent grey-blue foliage and in summer small yellow flower heads – a most striking plant for the small border. There's an unusual dwarf willow which would be suitable: *Salix lanata*, popularly called the woolly willow as a greyish white felt covers the leaves. Upright yellow catkins are produced in the spring. Grow both of these in a sunny spot.

A striking new dwarf shrub is *Spiraea japonica* 'Golden Princess' with brilliant golden foliage throughout the summer and bright pink flowers carried in flat heads in mid-summer. For best colour it should be grown in a sunny position.

63

Brightening Up A Dull Concrete Corner

An area of concrete, perhaps laid by a previous owner of the house, does not necessarily present a problem and it does not have to be broken up and lifted.

It is an easy matter to hide concrete by covering it with a layer of coloured gravel, which is available in various shades including white, black, grey and even pink. You could use several different colours to form a contrasting pattern, separating them, perhaps, with lines of bricks laid flat and cemented to the concrete. Certainly the edges of the area should be formed of bricks to prevent the gravel from spreading. An attractive surface could also be formed with coloured pebbles, say in shades of pink and grey, laid like cobbles and again cemented to the concrete base.

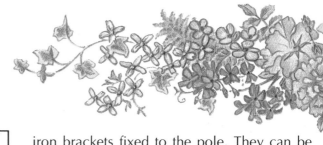

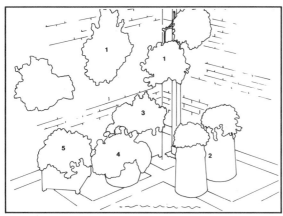

1. Hanging baskets filled with pendulous summer bedding plants
2. Bedding impatiens in chimney pots
3. Fuchsias
4. Pelargoniums, lobelia and alyssum
5. Petunias

COLOURFUL CONTAINERS

We now have an attractive base which could be used for various features. A collection of gaily painted square wooden tubs would further help to provide colour. Tubs painted red and white are particularly cheerful: for instance, have the corners and the cross pieces at the top and bottom picked out in red. Wooden barrels and half barrels could also be white, with the metal bands painted red. Fill these containers with brightly coloured bedding plants and bulbs, such as red pelargoniums for summer and scarlet tulips for spring.

A collection of hanging baskets on a pole would also form an unusual feature. A timber fencing post, again perhaps painted red or white, could be used, fixed to the concrete with a special metal post support. The baskets can be supported with ornamental wrought-iron brackets fixed to the pole. They can be filled with colourful trailing bedding plants for the summer, like petunias, lobelia, pendulous fuchsias and begonias, ivy-leaf pelargoniums and impatiens. For winter they could be planted with winter-flowering pansies and for spring with double daisies and polyanthus.

Some people collect old chimney pots and use them as garden features. Some are quite ornamental and invariably they are glazed. If these appeal to you, group a collection together in this corner, fill them with potting compost and plant with hanging-basket subjects (see above). Alternatively they make good supports for baskets – simply stand a basket on top of each chimney pot. Remove the chains from the baskets as these will not be needed, of course.

AN EYE-CATCHING FOLLY

Why not consider a folly for this corner? A folly is a structure designed to catch the eye, often bizarre or amusing, but with no functional purpose. Something which admirably fits the bill is the old red telephone box. Currently these boxes are being sold off and there is great demand for them, not only in Britain but in the USA as well. It seems that some people intend to install them in their gardens, not for any particular purpose but for sentimental reasons. Some buyers, though, have said they will use their box as a mini summerhouse; while others, it seems, will grow tomatoes in them, or other tender crops like sweet peppers or aubergines. In this instance, though, one would have to guard against rapid heating up in the summer by leaving the door open on warm days. In my view it is essential to keep these old telephone boxes bright red: any other colour would ruin their character. What better, then, to provide a bright splash of colour in a dull corner than the endearing British 'phone box?

CHAPTER FIVE

EASY MINI FEATURES

There are several small features, easily created and relatively inexpensive, that can be considered for corners. They will rapidly transform a dull and boring area into one that is both unusual and full of interest.

PLANT WHEELS

Attractive circular beds, perhaps even formed of old cartwheels, for displaying small herbs and other dwarf plants.

A RAISED BED

A raised bed fits well into a corner and is the ideal site for displaying trailing plants, or dwarf conifers and heathers.

SELF-CONTAINED WATER FEATURES

The sight and sound of moving water provided by one of the modern, self-contained water features (those which do not need a pool). Also a bog garden in a domestic cold-water tank, and a mini pool.

BEDDING WITH DWARF PERENNIALS

If you don't have the time for spring and summer bedding schemes, consider labour-saving permanent displays with dwarf hardy perennials.

A FOLIAGE CORNER

Creating a lush jungle-like effect with bold and dramatic, often bizarre, foliage plants, with contrast in shape, texture and colour. And not forgetting a statue.

Plant Wheels

The plant wheel is an unusual way of displaying small herbs and other dwarf plants, such as miniature roses, and it fits into any odd corner. A particularly good place for it, especially if filled with culinary herbs, would be outside the back door.

Basically the plant wheel consists of a circular bed divided into a number of segments, so that it looks like a wheel. Each segment is then planted with a different kind of plant.

The plant wheel can be formed of bricks which are simply laid on the soil surface. There is no need to set them permanently in place with mortar. Bricks can be laid on edge or flat.

Alternatively if you can find an old large wooden cartwheel you could use this after painting it a pleasing colour. Simply bed it down onto the soil and then plant between the spokes.

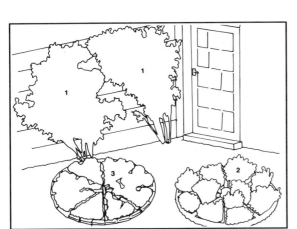

1. Climbing roses forming a colourful background
2. A bed of mixed herbs
3. A bed of miniature roses

I would suggest a sunny position with well-drained soil for this feature, especially if you want to grow herbs. A good place for a herb wheel would be near the kitchen door so that you can quickly nip out and gather a few herbs while you are preparing meals.

SOME USEFUL HERBS

Many herbs are very decorative, especially varieties of sage, *Salvia officinalis,* like the purple-leaved 'Purpurascens', the yellow-edged 'Icterina' and the multicoloured 'Tricolor'. The golden marjoram, *Origanum vulgare* 'Aureum', has attractive yellow leaves. Some of the mints are very decorative plants, especially the white and green variegated pineapple mint, *Mentha suaveolens* 'Variegata', and the golden variegated ginger mint, *M. × gentilis* 'Variegata'. Chives, *Allium schoenoprasum,* are attractive, too, especially when in flower: they produce heads of rose-purple blooms in the summer. The fresh green curly foliage of parsley, *Petroselinum*

crispum, a widely used herb, is most decorative. Rue, *Ruta graveolens,* has greyish or bluish foliage which is very pungent. In the past it was used as a medicinal herb but today is valued only as a decorative plant. For the best foliage colour try to obtain the variety 'Jackman's Blue' whose leaves are virtually blue. The thymes are attractive herbs and, of course, are widely used in cooking. The garden thyme, *Thymus vulgaris,* produces tiny lilac-mauve flowers in the summer and the lemon thyme, *T. × citriodorus,* has lemon-scented foliage and pink flowers in late summer. Grow any other favourite herbs, too, in your plant wheel, provided they are not tall kinds which would upset the balance of this comparatively low-growing feature.

A RAISED BED

A raised bed for displaying plants could be built into a corner and would be especially attractive if bow-fronted. Apart from making an attractive feature, a raised bed has several other advantages: it gives a change in level, especially important if your garden is perfectly flat; it allows you to provide special soil for any plants which need it (for example, acid soil for lime-hating plants like dwarf rhododendrons and azaleas); and it provides the perfect setting for trailing plants, which are allowed to cascade over the edges of the bed.

HOW TO BUILD

I would suggest a minimum height of 30 cm (12 in) and no more than 60 cm (24 in). A bed is easily built from bricks (ideally to match those of the house) or from ornamental concrete walling blocks which resemble natural stone. Alternatively you could use natural walling stone, either bonding it with mortar or laying it dry (know as dry-stone walling). The walls

should be built on a firm trench foundation consisting of a layer of hardcore topped with concrete. After building the bed the walls should be topped with coping stones.

If you want a more rustic effect build the raised bed with timber, such as proprietary log rolls which are made from half-round timber pales joined together with flexible metal strips. They are available in 1 m (39 in) lengths and can easily be joined together. The 30 or 45 cm (12 or 18 in) high log rolls are suitable for raised beds.

Fill the bed with good quality topsoil or with a soil-based potting compost. It can then be filled with plants of your choice: for instance, you may want a riot of colour as provided by summer bedding plants, and spring bedding plants and bulbs; or you may prefer a more labour-saving scheme and opt for permanent plants. There is a wide range of small and dwarf shrubs and perennials to choose from but if you want a particular theme why not opt for a bed of dwarf conifers and heathers, particularly suitable for a modern setting.

CONIFERS AND HEATHERS

Many dwarf conifers are highly colourful such as the deep gold *Thuja occidentalis* 'Rheingold'; the bright yellow *Chamaecyparis pisifera* 'Filifera Aurea'; the silvery blue *Chamaecyparis pisifera* 'Boulevard'; and the greyish or bluish green *Juniperus chinensis* 'Pyramidalis'. For the edges of the bed choose spreading or carpeting junipers like *Juniperus horizontalis* 'Banff' with brilliant silvery blue foliage or *J. h.* 'Blue Chip' with feathery foliage in a similar colour. Also with a spreading habit is *Juniperus × media* 'Gold Sovereign' with brilliant yellow foliage throughout the year.

Choose heathers for flowering at different times of the year. For winter I recommend varieties of *Erica herbacea (E. carnea)* and *E. × darleyensis,* with flowers in shades of pink, red and also white. For summer, varieties of *Calluna vulgaris* are virtually essential and colours include shades of pink, red, purple and white. Some varieties have golden or reddish foliage which is attractive all the year round, but particularly effective during the winter. Bear in mind that *Calluna vulgaris* varieties must have acid or lime-free soil, but this should present no problem with a raised bed. The winter-flowering heathers will tolerate lime or chalk in the soil.

Also flowering in the summer are varieties of *Daboecia cantabrica* (St. Dabeoc's heath) which are rather different from other heathers as they have quite large, elliptic leaves and also fairly large bell-shaped flowers. Varieties come in shades of pink, red, purple or white. Daboecias must be grown in acid soil which should not be prone to drying out. Varieties of *Erica cinerea* are also well worth growing for their summer display. Commonly known as bell heathers, the plants must be grown in acid soil. Some varieties have golden foliage which shows up especially well in the winter. I am particularly fond of *E. tetralix* and its varieties. It is commonly known as the cross-leaved heath and the foliage is grey or greyish-green. Summer flowering; must be grown in acid soil.

Erica vagans, the Cornish heath, has numerous varieties and flowers during the summer. Although it can be grown in slightly alkaline or chalky conditions it really does best in acid soils.

Some of the taller heathers could be planted to give additional height – not the true tree heaths as they are rather too tall for our purpose, but certainly species like *Erica erigena.* This is the Mediterranean heath, a bushy upright plant suitable for chalky soils.

To keep heathers neat and compact lightly trim them over with shears or scissors after flowering, just removing the dead flower heads.

Self-contained Water Features

The sight and sound of moving water greatly adds to the interest of a garden and what better for a small corner than one of the self-contained water features – in other words, those which do not need a pool.

One of the simplest, and also most popular, is the bubble fountain where water bubbles out of the central hole of an artificial 'millstone' (often made from glass-fibre) and trickles down the sides into a surround of cobbles or smooth pebbles. A small hidden reservoir holds the water which is circulated by a small pump. This can make a striking feature for a small patio, or it can be used on its own, surrounded by bold foliage and flowering plants such as hostas, rodgersias and astilbes.

1. Background of ivy (hedera)
2. *Typha minima* (reed mace)
3. *Mimulus cardinalis* (monkey flower)
4. *Caltha palustris* 'Plena' (double marsh marigold)
5. *Lysichitum camtschatcense* (skunk cabbage)
6. *Eriophorum angustifolium* (cotton grass)

There are many self-contained fountain units available from water-gardening specialists and garden centres. Most are in the form of statues and the water, which is circulated by means of a pump, falls into an integral bowl or dish. If you have only a small garden, don't be tempted to buy anything too elaborate or large as it can look rather pretentious. There are available, in fact, small cascade or fountain units which look like modern sculpture, ideally suited to small contemporary town gardens.

The water feature could be illuminated at night with a coloured garden spotlight.

MINI BOG GARDEN

Why not consider having a mini bog garden in a corner, in which to grow colourful and interesting moisture-loving plants? You will need a sunny position for this.

The bog garden can be made in a domestic

cold-water tank which can be bought from any builders' or plumbers' merchant. The tank should be filled with a heavy loamy topsoil. Water is added as necessary to keep the soil constantly moist or slightly wet, but never add so much that it becomes waterlogged.

There are lots of exciting and colourful bog plants that could be planted in this tank. The mimulus or monkey flowers provide brilliant colour during the summer. *M. cardinalis* has brilliant red flowers with a yellow centre; *M. guttatus* sports yellow flowers strikingly blotched with brown; *M. luteus* also has yellow blooms but they are heavily marked with crimson or maroon; and *M. ringens* has the most attractive light blue flowers which appear in late summer and early autumn.

Try the white skunk cabbage, *Lysichitum camtschatcense,* with large white sail-like flowers in the spring, followed by large, lush green foliage. A truly bizarre moisture-loving plant. Reed maces are also suitable for our tank, provided you choose the less-vigorous kinds like *Typha stenophylla* and *T. minima.* These produce amusing brown poker-like flowers and many people think they are bulrushes, but these are different plants and not recommended for tanks as they are too vigorous.

The golden-yellow flowers of the double marsh marigold, *Caltha palustris* 'Plena', are a welcome sight in spring. A rather more unusual and amusing bog plant is the cotton grass, *Eriophorum angustifolium,* with rush-like foliage and flower heads which resemble balls of cotton wool.

MINI POOL

Another idea for this corner is a mini pool for aquatic or water plants, created in a large wooden tub. In this could be grown a miniature waterlily and some attractive marginal or shallow-water aquatics, not forgetting sub-

HELPFUL HINTS

The mini bog garden will need little attention once planted. However, when stems and foliage have died down they should be cut off at soil level or just above the crowns of the plants. Bog plants, like other subjects, benefit from feeding; it is always a good idea for them to be given a sprinkling of granular flower-garden fertilizer in the spring just as they are starting into growth.

When the tank starts to become overcrowded it is time to lift the plants, divide them into smaller portions and replant. The best time to do this is in the spring just as the plants are starting into growth. Carefully lift the clumps, wash the soil from the roots and then pull them apart into hand-sized portions for replanting. The centre part of each clump is, of course, the oldest, and therefore declining in vigour, so should be discarded, leaving only the young, vigorous outer portions for replanting.

Replant the divisions immediately and make sure the roots do not dry out during this operation.

merged oxygenating plants to help keep the water clear.

You will need a fairly large wooden tub, say with a diameter of between 60 and 90 cm (2 and 3 ft), with a similar depth. Certainly the depth should not be less than 45 cm (18 in).

In all probability the tub will leak, so in this instance line it with a piece of black butyl-rubber pool liner.

Choose a sunny part of the corner for your mini pool and either simply stand it on a paved area or, perhaps even more attractive, sink it almost up to its rim in the ground. Then the edges can be hidden with flat pieces of rock, and small moisture-loving plants could be planted around the edges.

The next stage is to prepare the pool for planting. The plants are best grown in a layer of heavy (or 'clayey') loam placed in the bottom of the tub. It should be between 10 and 15 cm (4 and 6 in) deep. Also mound some loam up the sides of the tub to make a home for the marginal or shallow-water plants.

Now we come to the most exciting part: planting! A miniature waterlily could be planted in the centre of the tub. There are several miniature varieties, including *Nymphaea pygmaea alba* with white flowers; the deep pink *N. p.* 'Johann Pring'; and the beautiful soft-yellow *N. p. helvola.*

Now you should plant some bunches of submerged oxygenating plants or 'water weeds' to help keep the water clear. Among the best for tubs are species of myriophyllum or milfoil, with attractive feathery foliage.

Finally a few marginal plants can be planted around the sides of the tub, in the loam which has been mounded up for them. There are some highly attractive small marginal plants available, including *Acorus gramineus variegatus* with grassy yellow and green striped leaves. One of my great favourites is the double marsh marigold, *Caltha palustris* 'Plena', which has beautiful golden-yellow flowers in the spring. Then there's the bog bean, *Menyanthes trifoliata,* with pink flowers, and the arrowhead, *Sagittaria sagittifolia florepleno,* with double white blooms.

There's hardly room for fish in this mini pool, but it would be worth including some ramshorn snails as they feed on filamentous algae, which can quickly choke a small pool.

Bedding With Dwarf Perennials

Many people rely heavily on spring and summer bedding plants for providing colour in small beds and borders. This is fine if you have the time: you will certainly have continuous colour from early summer through into the autumn, and for much of the spring, too.

But temporary bedding schemes can take up a lot of time. Summer bedding plants have to be planted out in late spring or early summer, when the frosts are over; then they have to be cleared away when the display is over, usually around mid-autumn. Then immediately the spring bedding plants, and bulbs such as tulips, are planted. As soon as their display is over they have to be cleared to make way for summer bedding plants again.

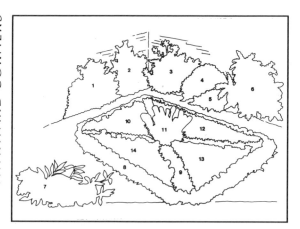

1. Hamamelis (witch hazel)
2. Pyracantha (firethorn)
3. Cotinus (smoke bush)
4. *Skimmia japonica* variety
5. Ground-cover cotoneaster
6. *Mahonia japonica*
7. *Euonymus europaeus* 'Red Cascade'.
8. *Prunella webbiana* variety
9. *Stachys lanata* 'Silver Carpet'
10. *Geranium* 'Johnson's Blue'
11. *Liatris callilepis*
12. *Polygonum affine* 'Dimity'
13. Erigeron hybrid
14. *Dianthus* 'Doris'

Two dwarf spring-flowering perennials for mass bedding. *Left: Pulsatilla vulgaris* (pasque flower) with purple or red flowers and ferny foliage. *Right: Ranunculus gramineus* (grass-leaved buttercup) with yellow blooms.

It is possible, though, to obtain equally colourful effects by creating permanent schemes with dwarf hardy perennials. These are mass-planted, in the same way as bedding plants, but will provide colour for years with minimum attention. All you have to do is cut down the dead stems in autumn and every four years lift and divide the plants and replant young portions. This is done in the early spring and results in better growth and flowering.

The dwarf perennials can be planted in bold groups or drifts in a bed. Really you can form any pattern desired, formal or informal, in the same way that bedding plants are used. The bed can be edged, if desired, with one particular subject, planting it in a broad band. The bed should be in a sunny corner for best results.

Choose perennials which grow no more than about 30 cm (12 in) in height; but if you want to vary the height of the scheme I suggest a group of a taller plant in the centre of the bed.

FOR SUMMER COLOUR

For a summer display choose from the following plants: *Anthemis cupaniana,* grey foliage and white daisy flowers; *Campanula lactiflora* 'Pouffe', light blue flowers; *Coreopsis grandiflora* 'Goldfink', yellow daisy flowers; *Dianthus* 'Doris', double rose-pink flowers; *Erigeron* hybrids, daisy-like flowers in various colours; *Geranium* 'Johnson's Blue', bright blue cup-shaped flowers; *Lychnis arkwrightii,* brilliant scarlet flowers; *Polygonum affine* 'Dimity', tiny pink poker-like flowers; *Prunella webbiana* varieties, pink or white flowers; *Solidago* 'Golden Thumb', yellow flowers; and *Stachys lanata* 'Silver Carpet', silver-grey

leaves if you want something taller for the centre of the bed choose bushy self-supporting plants with an upright habit such as *Oenothera* 'Highlight', yellow flowers, 60 cm (2 ft); *Liatris callilepis,* spikes of lilac-purple flowers, 90 cm (3 ft); or *Salvia superba* 'East Friesland', spikes of violet-purple flowers, 45 cm (18 in).

FOR SPRING COLOUR

A spring scheme could include *Bergenia* hybrids, large evergreen foliage and pink, red or white flowers; *Dicentra eximia,* pink flowers; *Doronicum* 'Spring Beauty', double yellow flowers; *Euphorbia epithymoides,* acid-yellow flowers; *Lamium maculatum* varieties, pink or white flowers, handsome foliage; *Primula denticulata,* mauve, purple, red or white flowers in globular heads; *Pulmonaria saccharata* varieties, blue; red, pink or white flowers; *Pulsatilla vulgaris,* purple or red flowers, attractive ferny foliage; and *Ranunculus gramineus,* yellow buttercup flowers. Taller plants for the centre include *Ranunculus acris* 'Flore Pleno' with yellow double flowers, 60 cm (2 ft); or *Trollius* hybrids with globe-shaped flowers in shades of orange and yellow, about 60 cm (2 ft).

COLOURFUL BACKGROUNDS

Of course, as with bedding schemes, there are seasons when the bed will provide no colour, so if possible include in the vicinity plants which have interest when the bed is out of flower, such as shrubs with autumn leaf colour, with winter flowers, or with autumn and winter berries and fruits. These could be used as a backing for the bed.

To give a few examples, one of the best shrubs for autumn leaf colour is the smoke bush, *Cotinus coggygria* 'Flame', whose foliage takes on brilliant orange tints. Excellent for autumn fruits is a spindle bush, *Euonymus*

Europaeus 'Red Cascade'. The foliage colour is eye-catching, too. You should also certainly include a cotoneaster for autumn and winter berries, such as *C.* 'Exburiensis' with orange-yellow berries.

There is no shortage of shrubs with winter flowers and among the most popular and colourful are the witch hazels or hamamelis. A great favourite is *H. mollis* 'Pallida' with large sulphur-yellow flowers. *H. m.* 'Goldcrest' can also be recommended — it has large golden-yellow blooms. There are some good varieties of *H. × intermedia,* too, like the coppery red 'Diane' and 'Jelena', and the light sulphur-yellow 'Moonlight' with quite fragrant flowers. 'Allgold' is deep yellow, while 'Carmine Red' has rather large light bronze blooms.

Or you might prefer an evergreen mahonia for winter flowers. One of the finest is *M. japonica,* with bold foliage and deliciously scented trusses of lemon-yellow blooms. Equally as good is *M.* 'Charity', also well-scented.

The evergreen laurustinus, *Viburnum tinus,* flowers in winter and spring, the heads of white flowers showing up well against the dark green foliage.

Garrya elliptica is another winter-flowering shrub. It has a good covering of evergreen foliage and bears rather unusual flowers – they are in the form of long greyish-green catkins. Even better is its variety 'James Roof' which has extra long catkins. It is worth noting that garrya is suitable for growing against a shady north-facing wall. In this situation a marvellous companion for this shrub is the winter-flowering jasmine, *Jasminum nudiflorum,* which bedecks itself with masses of bright yellow flowers in the winter.

Another excellent winter-flowering shrub is *Daphne mezereum* with the most sweetly-scented, purplish red flowers which start to appear in late winter.

A Foliage Corner

To create a lush jungle-like effect in corners I can recommend planting schemes consisting of bold and dramatic foliage plants. This is particularly suitable for small modern town gardens because foliage has a softening effect when associated with architecture and paving.

Do not think that a group of foliage plants is dull and uninteresting. Far from it: one can create some stunning contrasts in shape, texture and colour. Leaves come in all shapes and sizes: for instance, there are large hand-shaped leaves and attractive grassy and sword-shaped leaves. Some leaves are smooth and shiny while others are hairy or woolly, or deeply veined. Colours vary tremendously: there are all shades of green, grey and 'blue', yellow, gold, bronze and variegated (for example, white and green or yellow and green).

1. *Vitis coignetiae* (Japanese crimson glory vine)
2. *Miscanthus sacchariflorus*
3. *Hedera* (ivy)
4. *Aralia elata* (Japanese angelica tree)
5. *Fatsia japonica*
6. *Hosta sieboldiana* 'Elegans' (plantain lily)
7. *Miscanthus sinensis* 'Zebrinus' (zebra grass)
8. *Phormium* (New Zealand flax)

To create a really stunning planting scheme you should choose plants which contrast well in shape, texture and colour. A good selection of foliage plants has been described below. Do make sure that all the plants chosen for a corner will thrive in the particular conditions. For instance, if the corner is shady then all plants must be shade tolerant; if it is sunny then use only sun-loving plants.

Stone or reconstituted-stone statuary associates beautifully with foliage plants, so consider choosing a suitable figure for this scheme. Ideally it should be a light colour – white or a light stone shade – so that it shows up well, and give it a background of dark-coloured foliage.

At night garden lighting will very much enhance a foliage group for the textures of the leaves will be emphasized. I would use natural lighting but by all means use coloured lights if

preferred, such as blue or green.

There is a very wide range of dramatic, unusual and even bizarre foliage plants, so let's take a look at some of them.

GRASSY AND SWORD-LIKE FOLIAGE

Some of the most exciting foliage plants have grassy or sword-like leaves. One of my great favourites is a red-hot poker, *Kniphofia caulescens*. This species produces clumps of greyish leaves up to 90 cm (3 ft) long, broad and grassy. These are spectacular enough, but as a bonus 1.2 m (4 ft) high spikes of light salmon-red flowers are produced in the autumn. This, and indeed other red-hot pokers, must be grown in a sunny position.

There are many ornamental grasses that one could use in this group, such as the popular gardener's garters, *Phalaris arundinacea* 'Picta', with white and green striped leaves. It grows to about 60 cm (2 ft) in height and is rather vigorous so you will have to fork out surplus growth when it starts to encroach onto other plants. The zebra grass, *Miscanthus sinensis* 'Zebrinus', has yellow-banded leaves and grows to a height of about 1.2 m (4 ft). If you want a giant grass, say for the back of the group, then choose *Miscanthus sacchariflorus* which attains 3 m (10 ft) in height. The medium green leaves have an arching habit. The ornamental grasses need to be grown in a sunny position.

Bamboos are, of course, grassy plants and a very attractive species is *Arundinaria viridistriata* with purplish canes (or stems) and leaves which are boldly striped with bright yellow and green. It grows to a height of about 1.2 m (4 ft). The black bamboo, *Phyllostachys nigra*, has black canes up to 6 m (20 ft) in height and deep green foliage. Bamboos can be grown in sun or partial shade.

A most unusual dwarf grassy plant, for the

front of a group, is *Ophiopogon planiscapus* 'Nigrescens' with black foliage. It attains only about 15 cm (6 in) in height and grows well in sun or partial shade. It looks superb with plants which have variegated leaves.

Coming on to plants with sword-like leaves, we must include the phormiums or New Zealand flaxes, which are very fashionable, especially with owners of modern town gardens. If you want tall varieties, up to about 2 m (6 ft) in height, choose *Phormium tenax* 'Purpureum' with purplish foliage, or the green and yellow striped *P. t.* 'Variegatum'. Lower-growing kinds, not over 90 cm (3 ft) in height, include *P. cookianum* 'Cream Delight' with cream and green striped leaves; and *P. tenax* varieties 'Maori Sunrise' with bronze and pink foliage, 'Sundowner' with grey-purple, cream and pink leaves, and 'Yellow Wave' whose leaves are striped with deep yellow and green. The phormiums need a sheltered position in full sun and well-drained soil.

The leaves of *Yucca whipplei* are tipped with really sharp spines so treat the plant with respect! Established plants produce spikes of greenish-white lily-like flowers in summer.

Needing the same conditions as phormiums are the yuccas. When established these produce tall spikes of lily-like flowers in the summer. *Y. filamentosa* is interesting as it has white threads on the edges of its leaves. The flower spike grows up to 2 m (6 ft) in height. There is a variegated form, 'Variegata', whose leaves are striped with yellow and green. Well-known is Adam's needle, *Y. gloriosa*, which as it ages forms a thick tree-like stem carrying at the top a rosette of leaves, each of which is tipped with a really sharp spine. Flower spikes up to 2 m (6 ft) high are produced in summer. One of my favourite yuccas is *Y. whipplei*, similarly armed with spines. It produces a rosette of stiff greyish leaves and spikes of greenish white flowers on stems up to 2 m (6 ft) in height.

BROAD FOLIAGE

Other plants have large broad leaves and these contrast well with grassy or sword-like plants. Among the hardy perennials one must include hostas or plantain lilies. They are low-growing herbaceous plants with spikes of lily-like flowers in summer, but primarily they are foliage plants. Leaves come in all shades of green while others are greyish or bluish, yellow or gold and variegated. There are many to choose from but some of my favourites include 'Big Daddy', large blue leaves; *H. fortunei* 'Aurea', yellow foliage; 'Frances Williams', grey-green variegated with beige; 'Golden Medallion', golden foliage; *H. sieboldiana* 'Elegans', large blue-green leaves; and *H. ventricosa* 'Variegata', white and green variegated leaves. You will have to buy these varieties from a perennial-plant specialist as you are unlikely to find them as yet in garden centres. Hostas thrive in shade or sun and must be protected from slugs by placing slug pellets around them as soon as they start into growth in the spring.

Rodgersias often have large hand-shaped

One of the best species of rodgersia is *Rodgersia pinnata* with hand-shaped dark green leaves, growing to about 1.2m (4ft) in height. Best grown in partial shade.

leaves and are best suited to a position in partial shade. One of the best species is *R. pinnata* with dark green foliage and it grows to a height of about 1.2 m (4 ft). Even more attractive is the variety 'Superba' with bronze-coloured foliage. Like the hostas, rodgersias flourish best in moist soil.

Shrubs which can be recommended for the foliage corner include *Fatsia japonica* with large, evergreen, deep green glossy leaves and heads of white flowers in the autumn. It is quite a large shrub, 2.4–3.6 m (8–12 ft) in height and spread and it requires a sheltered corner which can be sunny or shady.

The Japanese angelica tree, *Aralia elata,* is a rather unusual deciduous shrub 4 m (13 ft) or more in height. It produces a few upright spiny stems bearing massive compound leaves and large heads of white flowers in summer. Sun or partial shade.

For really large heart-shaped leaves grow *Paulownia tomentosa* as a shrub (really it's a large tree) by cutting the stems down to ground each year in early spring. The resultant shoots may need thinning out and can attain a height of at least 2 m. Needs sun and a sheltered spot.

A fun plant is the corkscrew hazel, *Corylus avellana* 'Contorta', with twisted branches and shoots which show up particularly well in the winter. Yellow catkins are produced on the bare branches in late winter/early spring. Really this is grown more for its stems than for its broad oval green leaves. Can be grown in sun or partial shade.

Finally, a dramatic climber which you could grow on the wall or fence in this 'jungle corner': the Japanese crimson glory vine, *Vitis coignetiae.* It has large lobed leaves which are most spectacular in autumn when they turn to shades of yellow, orange and crimson. It is a very vigorous tall climber but can be restrained by pruning in the autumn when the leaves have fallen. Suitable for sun or partial shade.

CHAPTER SIX

COLLECTORS' CORNERS

If you like collecting particular groups of plants, there are various ways of displaying them attractively and appropriately in corners of the garden.

RAISED PEAT BEDS

A partially shady corner provides the right setting for a raised peat bed in which can be grown plants that like lime-free soil, such as dwarf rhododendrons.

———

DISPLAYING ALPINES

An unusual way of displaying alpines is in a scree bed, which imitates a drift of broken rock at the base of a cliff. A mini rock garden can also be created in a stone sink.

If you have a partially shady corner (say dappled shade created by a tree) you might like to consider having raised peat beds for plants which like acid or lime-free, cool moist soil, such as dwarf rhododendrons. The beds are built up with peat blocks and filled with a peaty soil mixture.

This is still quite a novel idea in the UK, but is well known and very popular in the USA. The idea is particularly suitable for a modern town garden as peat beds are quite formal in design.

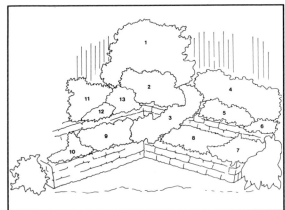

1. *Berberidopsis corallina* (coral plant)
2. *Rhododendron campylogynum*
3. *Arctostaphyllos uva-ursi*
4. *Rhododendron* 'Temple Belle'
5. *Rhododendron forrestii repens*
6. *Gaultheria procumbens*
7. *Lithospermum diffusum*
8. *Cassiope lycopodioides*
9. *Rhododendron impeditum*
10. *Gaultheria procumbens*
11. *Rhododendron* 'Elizabeth'
12. *Cassiope lycopodioides*
13. *Lithospermum diffusum*

BUILDING THE BEDS

The peat beds can be built like a series of terraces against a wall; but they must not be built against the wall of the house, garage or other outbuilding as they would be above the damp-proof course. If necessary, build a special retaining wall for this feature, using cheap bricks or concrete building blocks.

The minimum depth for each bed should be 45 cm (18 in), especially if your garden soil is alkaline (limy or chalky). However, if your garden soil is acid, you could get away with a minimum depth of 30 cm (12 in).

As can be seen in the drawing, the terraces are built up with peat blocks. These are formed of compressed peat and are about the size of house bricks. They are very dry when delivered so they must be soaked in water for at least 24 hours before use. When building with peat blocks you should stagger them like bricks in a wall, and the walls should tilt slightly inwards to make them really stable. When laying the peat blocks fill the joints with compost (the formula is given later) in the same way as you would use mortar when laying normal bricks, except that the compost is only slightly moist.

When building a series of terraces as shown here, complete the lower one first, filling it with compost, then build the second one on top.

However, before filling a bed with compost, place an 8 cm (3 in) layer of coarse peat over the garden soil. It would be advisable to dig the soil first and then to firm it by treading.

A suitable compost for peat beds consists of 4 parts moist sphagnum peat, 1 part fibrous acid (lime-free) loam and 1 part lime-free coarse sand (parts by volume). It should be firmed moderately, either with your hands or by treading lightly.

When the beds have been planted, the compost surface should be covered with about 2.5 cm (1 in) of sphagnum peat. As this decomposes it should be topped up (this may be needed annually). It is very important, during dry weather, to keep peat beds watered as they must not be allowed to dry out. Equally important is keeping the peat blocks permanently moist to prevent them drying out and shrinking.

The ground around the peat terraces can be covered as desired, but I would suggest a layer of coarse pulverized bark as this is in-keeping with this particular theme. It makes an attractive surface which is soft and spongy to walk on. What I particularly like about bark is that it gives off a delicious woody smell when

wet, adding to the pleasures of the garden.

PEAT-GARDEN PLANTS

There are quite a few delightful peat-garden plants that you could use. Bear in mind that all plants should, ideally, be dwarf and restrained in habit to prevent them from quickly outgrowing the beds and, indeed, swamping neighbouring plants. Any which have a low spreading habit are best planted at the edges of the beds so that they trail down over the sides.

Dwarf rhododendrons
Probably the most popular plants for peat beds are the dwarf rhododendron species and hybrids, of which there are many to choose from. For a really good choice you should buy from a rhododendron specialist, although these days garden centres do carry a reasonably good selection, mainly hybrids.

Some attractive dwarf rhododendron species include *R. forrestii repens,* a prostrate grower with bell-shaped flowers in vivid scarlet; *R. campylogynum,* also with bell-shaped blooms, but this time in shades of pink or purple, depending on the form; and *R. impeditum,* a beautiful little species forming a low mound of minute leaves and bearing small purplish-blue flowers.

There are so many dwarf rhododendron hybrids that it is really a case of choosing those which appeal to you. I am particularly fond of *R.* 'Temple Belle' which has bell-shaped blooms in rose-pink on a compact, rounded bush; and *R.* 'Elizabeth', which smothers itself with trumpet-shaped blooms in brilliant deep red.

Other choice plants
Other plants that I recommend you consider include cassiopes which are small, neat, evergreen shrubs producing in spring white bell-shaped flowers. They are all very similar but I suggest you look out for the species *C. lycopodioides* and *C. tetragona.*

A superb small spreading sub-shrub valued for its vivid, pure blue flowers in summer and autumn is *Lithospermum diffusum.* Try to obtain the variety 'Heavenly Blue'.

A prostrate, spreading evergreen shrub, of restrained habit, is *Arctostaphyllos uva-ursi,* ideal for planting at the edge of a bed. In the spring this plant produces white urn-shaped flowers and these are followed by red berries.

Another spreading evergreen shrub is the checker-berry, *Gaultheria procumbens,* which should be planted at the edge of a bed, where it will not swamp other plants (it is quite a wide spreader). The foliage is deep green but takes on reddish tints in autumn, and the plant produces crops of brilliant red berries.

Another prostrate creeping shrub is *Vaccinium praestans,* with small bell-shaped blooms in early summer, which may be white or reddish, and these are followed by red berries. In the autumn the foliage takes on brilliant tints before it falls.

A rather unusual peat garden plant is *Parochetus communis,* a carpeting perennial, rather clover-like in general appearance but sporting bright blue, pea-like flowers in summer and autumn. Unfortunately it is not reliably hardy in areas subjected to hard winters.

If you want a climber to hide the back wall then choose one that enjoys the conditions provided by the peat bed. One that admirably fits the bill, and a most unusual plant, is *Berberidopsis corallina,* the coral plant. This is an evergreen climber with thick, deep green prickly leaves. Towards the end of the summer dangling dark crimson flowers are produced at the tips of the shoots. You may have to buy this from a specialist tree and shrub nurseryman as it is unlikely to be available from garden centres.

Displaying Alpines

Among the most popular groups of collectors' plants are alpines or rock plants. Such is their popularity that there is a society devoted to them which boasts a very large membership and holds shows throughout the country. There is no need to have a large rock garden though, to grow alpines. Indeed, you do not even need a rock garden. Consider growing them in a scree bed – imitating a drift of broken rocks. It is very easy and economical to construct. Another unusual way of displaying alpines is in stone sinks, so consider this idea as well for the alpine corner.

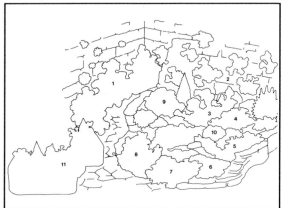

1. *Pinus mugo* 'Gnom' (dwarf pine)
2. Lewisias
3. *Saxifraga cochlearis* (saxifrage)
4. *Gentiana septemfida* (gentian)
5. *Dianthus alpinus* (alpine pink)
6. Draba species
7. *Leontopodium alpinum* (edelweiss)
8. Androsace species
9. Sedum species
10. Veronica species
11. Stone sinks planted with alpines

A SCREE BED

Many people like to collect alpines or rock plants and an appropriate way of displaying them is on a rock garden. However, this is quite expensive to construct and a fair amount of skill is required if it is to look natural. A more unusual way of displaying alpines is in a scree bed, which is very easy to construct.

But what is a scree bed? In nature a scree is a drift or layer of broken rock at the bottom of a rock face or cliff. It builds up as the cliff is eroded by the weather. In a natural scree plants that like very well drained, sparse conditions flourish, for there is little in the way of soil or nutrients.

In the garden we can grow similar alpines in a scree, which makes a very attractive feature in a sunny corner.

Most people create a scree without the rock face or cliff behind, but I do not see why we should not build a mini cliff to create a more authentic effect. It does not have to be too high, as we are not trying to copy nature exactly. To build a cliff, rectangular rocks are stacked one on top of the other. Place hard stones between the rocks to keep them apart and fill these joints with compost. You can then plant suitable alpines in these joints, such as lewisias. For stability, the cliff should slope slightly in towards the wall. Never build a cliff against the wall of the house, garage or other building as it will be above the damp-proof course. If you do not have a suitable wall against which to build, then it might be worthwhile building one specially for this feature, using cheap bricks or concrete building blocks (they will, after all, be hidden).

Then the scree bed is created at the base of the cliff, making it slope from the back to the front. It should be built on soil and the edges can be retained as necessary with more rocks. Make the scree bed of irregular shape.

The bed is built up with a well-drained compost which you can make at home. It consists of 10 parts stone chippings or pea shingle, 1 part loam, 1 part peat and 1 part sharp horticultural sand (parts by volume). Add a little organic slow-release fertilizer such as bonemeal. This mixture is placed over the soil, after covering the ground with a 10 cm (4 in) layer of broken bricks or rubble to ensure good drainage. The minimum depth of the compost should be 30 cm (12 in); it will, of course, be deeper towards the back – perhaps up to 60 cm (2 ft). After planting, the scree bed can be covered with a layer of stone chippings.

Choosing plants
There are many alpines which enjoy the

conditions provided by a scree bed. You can even grow those which are considered to be difficult on a normal rock garden due to the fact that they need really good drainage. You will have to buy most alpines, especially the choice ones, from a specialist grower as garden centres only stock the most popular kinds.

Alpines for a scree bed include species of the following: *Androsace, Calceolaria, Daphne, Dianthus, Draba, Gentiana, Hebe, Iris, Leontopodium* (the popular edelweiss), *Lewisia* (also suitable for the cliff face), *Phyteuma, Saxifraga* (there are dozens of species of saxifrages), *Sedum, Teucrium* and *Veronica*. A good alpine specialist's catalogue will tell you which species are most suitable for a scree bed.

The scree bed can be surrounded with gravel, which looks quite natural, or with random-stone or 'crazy' paving.

To further help create the right atmosphere, plant some dwarf pines in the vicinity of the scree bed, such as *Pinus mugo* 'Gnom'. Pines are often found growing in mountainous country.

STONE SINKS

Another way of displaying alpines is in stone sinks placed on a paved or gravelled area, again in a sunny corner.

Ideally try to obtain the old-fashioned shallow stone sinks. These are quite scarce and are considered collectors' items, so you will have to be prepared to hunt around for them and to pay quite high prices.

If you cannot find or afford to buy genuine old stone sinks then you should consider converting a white glazed sink so that it resembles natural stone. These are readily available from local builders or scrap yards as many people are discarding them in favour of fitted designer kitchens.

The sink is covered with a mixture of cement, sand and peat, known as hypertufa. When it becomes hard and has started to weather, it resembles natural tufa rock, which is a soft limestone.

Before applying a hypertufa mix, the surface of the sink has to be treated with a PVA adhesive to ensure the hypertufa sticks to the shiny glaze. PVA adhesive (which is used in the building trade) is available from hardware and DIY stores. Use a brush and apply it to the outside of the sink and several inches down on the inside. The hypertufa mix is applied when the adhesive has become tacky, before it is fully dry.

A hypertufa mix can be made up as follows: 1 part cement, 1 part sand and 2 parts sphagnum peat (parts by volume). Then add enough water to make a stiff but pliable mix.

This mix is spread all over the treated area of the sink, about 12 mm (1/2 in) thick, pressing it firmly into place with your fingers. The surface of the hypertufa should be left fairly rough so that it resembles natural stone.

Now the sink should be left alone for a couple of weeks to allow the hypertufa to thoroughly harden. Then fill the sink with a solution of permanganate of potash for a day or so as this will remove chemicals from the cement, which could be harmful to plants. Finally thoroughly wash out the sink with plain water.

Sinks can be stood on two rows of bricks, two courses high, to raise them nearer the eye, and the bricks should be bonded with mortar. Once the sinks are in place fill them with a suitable compost, but first put a layer of drainage material in the bottom. 'Crocks' or broken clay flower pots make the best drainage material. First place a large piece over the drainage hole and then spread a 2.5 cm (1 in) layer of crocks over the bottom of the sink. Cover these with a thin layer of leafmould or rough peat.

93

Use a soil-based potting compost for alpines but add one-third extra of coarse horticultural sand or grit to make sure that it drains really well. Fill the sinks to within 2.5 cm (1 in) of the top with this compost.

Some small pieces of natural rock bedded into the compost will create a pleasing effect, especially when some of the alpines start to creep over them.

Choosing plants

One has to choose restrained alpines for sinks as very vigorous kinds would quickly fill it and swamp each other. You will need to create some height in the planting scheme, as alpines are low-growing or prostrate plants. So first plant a little group of dwarf conifers. Highly recommended is the Noah's ark juniper, *Juniperus communis* 'Compressa', which forms a greyish-green cone. It is very slow-growing.

We need trailing plants for the edges of the sinks and there are quite a few to choose from, like the spring-flowering *Phlox douglasii* which produces sheets of lilac flowers. Also very floriferous, producing pink flowers in early summer, is *Aethionema armenum*. I am particularly fond of the mat-forming raoulias

and can recommend *R. hookeri* which forms a silver carpet with its minute leaves.

Then in the rest of the sink plant hummock- or mound-forming alpines, of compact habit, like the saxifrages with white, yellow, pink or red flowers, mainly in spring. The sempervivums or houseleeks would also be suitable and are grown mainly for their attractive succulent leaves rather than flowers. Rather amusing is the cobweb houseleek, *Sempervivum arachnoideum,* which is covered with white webbing. A thrift could be included, like *Armeria caespitosa,* with pink blooms in spring; and certainly the rock pink, *Dianthus neglectus,* with rose-pink blooms in early summer. Also with pink blooms, but in the spring, is *Geranium cinereum.* Alpine gypsophilas are also recommended, such as *G. caucasica,* which has dainty white flowers in early summer. One could go on, but if you are an enthusiastic alpine collector you will no doubt have your own treasures that you will want to include in sinks.

After planting your sinks cover the surface of the compost with stone chippings to create an attractive appearance. Chippings also help to ensure good drainage around the plants.

INDEX

ACKNOWLEDGEMENTS

Illustrations on pages 1, 3, 8, 12, 16, 36, 40, 48 & 64 are by Cheryl Wilbraham (*The Garden Studio*).
Illustrations on pages 5, 14, 19, 22, 28, 34, 43, 48, 63, 77, 78, 83, 84, 87 & 91 are by Cynthia Pow.
Illustrations on pages 26, 30, 44, 52, 56, 60, 68, 72 & 80 are by Jane Pickering (*Linden Artists*).